FOOD as GIFTS

Delicious ideas for presents to suit all occasions.

FOOD as GIFTS

'Simply delicious presents for all occasions'

JO MARCANGELO

THORSONS PUBLISHING GROUP

First published 1988

© JO MARCANGELO 1988

British Library Cataloguing in Publication Data

Marcangelo, Jo
Food as gifts.
1. Cookery
I. Title
641.5'68   TX717

ISBN 0-7225-1647-9

Published by Thorsons Publishers Limited,
Wellingborough, Northamptonshire, NN8 2RQ, England.

Printed in Great Britain by Hazell Watson & Viney Limited,
Member of BPCC plc, Aylesbury, Bucks

1   3   5   7   9   10   8   6   4   2

Contents

Introduction

Home-made presents mean so much more than shop-bought gifts and, if your talent lies in cooking, what better gifts than those from your kitchen? Practically everyone, young and old, can be given an edible gift and if you are imaginative about the container, this becomes a secondary present. A prettily wrapped box of hand-made sweets, a jar of pickled walnuts, a bottle of raspberry-flavoured wine vinegar — all will have the personal touch that only making a present yourself can give.

This book offers a wide selection of preserves, pickles, pâtés, biscuits, cakes, teabreads, sweets and fruits steeped in alcohol, with the added bonus that they are made from only the best natural ingredients and are free from artificial preservatives and additives. Whether you're making them for friends and relatives or to raise money at a charity bazaar, you'll find these recipes will provide you with a delicious variety.

Happy giving!

Presentation Gifts

Everyone welcomes a home-made gift that is good to eat or drink and is attractively presented. A single jar of conserve or a bottle of flavoured wine vinegar can make a very attractive present. However, pretty or inventive packaging or wrapping can enhance the sense of occasion and 'specialness'. Why not put your present in a useful container? Give an apron, its pockets filled with two jars of home-made jam; an attractive plate spread with a selection of home-made sweets; a vase or pottery mug piled high with fruit and nut clusters; or a chunky preserving jar for pickled walnuts with a pickle spoon attached to its side which can be enjoyed long after the edibles have been eaten.

Home-made gift containers and decorations need not be expensive. With a little time, patience and imagination you can create extremely pretty packaging by making use of existing containers and materials. The following pages will, I hope, give you some useful ideas. Always store goods in airtight containers or the refrigerator and gift wrap them at the last minute.

Labels

It is important to give plenty of information on the labels of food presents. Always put the date of making on labels for preserves, pâtés, spreads, potted cheese or anything that has to be kept in the refrigerator. This should ensure that the food is eaten while it is still in prime condition. Add instructions for use wherever these might be necessary. Use chic red sealing wax and red ribbons to attach a label to a bottle.

Collecting containers

Make a habit of collecting interesting jars and bottles. Save boxes of all sizes — bought ones can be expensive. Other useful containers include shallow foil dishes, disposable plastic and polystyrene pots and trays used for dairy products and vegetables, but take care if reusing containers as they harbour strong smells which could seep into your prize offering. Cover with paper or material, add some decorative adhesive shapes and finish with bows (the ready-tied adhesive ones are handy) and ribbons. And don't forget to save all the brightly coloured wrapping paper, card, material and ribbons that come your way too.

Glasses

Small tumblers and glasses make excellent containers for fruit butters and savoury spreads (such as peanut or cashew butter), as well as for spiced nuts and seeds. Cocktail-type stemmed glasses make novel containers for truffles and sweets with a bow tied round the top of the stem.

Jars and bottles

Many of my jars and bottles come from junk or second-hand shops. I have made a habit of looking through those boxes labelled '50p and under' and have found some treasures — old-fashioned preserving jars with blue-green glass lids and also bottles with a decorative frieze in the glass. The rubber rings to use with these old jars are still widely available, but check old jars carefully to make sure that they or their rings are not cracked or chipped. If they are, the jar will not form an airtight seal. Corks can be bought from home-brew shops and whittled down to fit any bottle without its top.

Fabric

Make pretty mob-caps for jams and pickles from odd scraps of material. Use cheerful bold checked or plain fabric for pickles, relishes and chutneys and very pretty patterns for conserves, curds or fruit in alcohol. Find something of suitable size for a pattern to draw round. For a special effect, cut round the edges with pinking shears. Tie with knitting wool, fine cord, ribbon or coloured string, but not elastic bands which easily get pushed off. Alternatively, you can wrap bottles and jars completely in fabric, gathering it around the neck with ribbon and finishing off with a bow.

Tea-towels
Tea-towels, in bright colours and cheerful designs, make delightful wrappings. They are particularly well suited to cakes (which should first be wrapped in foil or non-PVC cling-film) and, when tied round with ribbon, look like miniature parcels.

Baskets
Wicker baskets come in all shapes and sizes. Small baskets with hooped handles make delightful containers for transporting jars of conserve. Stick broderie anglaise or lace inside the basket rim to create a pretty frill all the way round. Twine ribbon around the handle and finish at each end with a small bow. Cut the ends of the ribbon into 'swallow tails'.

Boxes
Boxes in all shapes, colours and sizes are now available in good stationers and department stores. One of the simplest ways of making your gift wrappings distinctive is, of course, to re-cover existing boxes; chocolate or writing paper boxes with lids are particularly useful. To cover a box with gift paper, open up the box, separating the glued joins, and trace round the flat box, adding ½ inch (1cm) all round. Spread glue on the extra ½ inch (1cm) and fold it onto the flat box. Leave to dry, then glue the box back together again.

The plans for a rectangular and a cube-shaped box are shown on pages 12 and 13. The measurements given are only very basic guidelines, as the final size of the box is dictated by what you wish to put inside it. The cube box is easier, since only one measurement is required for all the straight edges. Use a ruler to draw up the plan on the card, and make sure that all the angles are right angles, or your box will look very strange when folded up.

Ribbons and bows
A decorative bow can give your box a professional finish. Make them from paper gift ribbon which can be moistened and pressed together to secure, and choose a colour that is complementary to your box. Do remember that they don't always have to sit glued to the centre of a box; try a rectangle with a bow at one end or at the corner. The most common width used is ¾ inch (2cm). Use real woven satin ribbons to tie gifts when you know the recipient will appreciate the ribbon as a 'second' gift.

To make a figure of eight bow: cut a length of ribbon approximately 24 inches (60cm) in length. Loop into a figure of eight at one end and secure at the centre. Repeat twice with the remaining ribbon, making each figure of eight slightly smaller than the previous one. Turn the end piece underneath to secure.

To make a star rosette: cut two lengths of ribbon approximately 16 inches (40cm) in length. Loop half the first length of ribbon into a figure of eight, giving each loop a half twist and moistening at the centre to hold. Repeat with the remaining half, but positioning the loops at right angles to the first two. Do the same with the second length. Fix one in place diagonally on top of the other and secure at the centre.

To make a tailored or flat loop bow: cut ribbon into 12, 10, 8 and 6 inch (30, 25, 20 and 15cm) lengths. Dampen the ends and form the pieces into rings. Flatten the rings and dampen inside to form double loops. Stick loops one on another, the longest at the bottom, the smallest on top. Make a small loop on top to finish.

Accessories
Keep the following handy:
kitchen foil
Sellotape
tissue paper in assorted colours
non-PVC cling-film (film wrap)
cake frills
ready-made rosettes
paper or fabric flowers
PVA glue
fabric for covering jars, such as gingham, floral printed cotton, etc.
paper doilies
assorted ribbons, cord and coloured string
braids
paper petit four cases for sweets in brown, white and floral designs
Cellophane paper by the roll
pretty and decorative labels
card — white or coloured (such as is sold for making greeting cards) for making tie-on
    labels and boxes

Flower-petal jar holder

1 Enlarge the pattern (see below) according to the size of the jar.

2 Place the pattern on the reverse side of patterned or plain card (stuck with patterned paper if wished). Outline and cut out.

3 Score and fold where shown on the plan (dotted lines indicate glue tabs, to be folded; broken lines indicate fold lines). Fold tabs and glue the box together.

4 Curve petals outward by rolling them over the inside of a roll of kitchen foil, a similar cardboard tube or a drinking glass. Tie ribbons or yarn around the neck to secure.

Materials
card (patterned or plain)
glue

Tools
scissors
steel rule
craft knife
pencil

Flower-petal jar holder

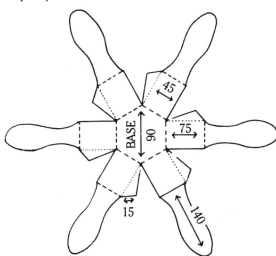

all dimensions in millimetres

11

Cube box

Materials
card (patterned or plain)
glue

Tools
steel rule
craft knife
pencil

1 Enlarge the pattern (see below) according to the gift size.
2 Place the pattern on the reverse side of patterned or plain card (stuck with patterned paper, if wished). Draw the outline and cut out the pattern using a steel rule and a craft knife.
3 Score the parts to be folded (shown on the pattern by broken lines). Glue A to B and leave to dry. Fold in the remaining tabs and the lid and base at the top and bottom. Decorate as wished.

Cube box
Fold along the broken lines

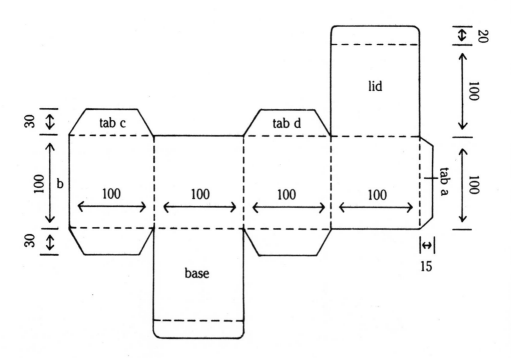

all dimensions in millimetres

12

Rectangular box

1 Enlarge the pattern (see below) according to gift size.
2 Place pattern on reverse side of patterned or plain card (stuck with patterned paper, if wished). Draw the outline and cut along all of the solid lines.
3 Score the parts to be folded (shown on the plan by broken lines) and fold the box into shape folding the tabs in alphabetical order. Decorate as required.

Materials
card (patterned or plain)
glue

Tools
steel rule
craft knife
pencil

Rectangular box
Fold along the broken lines

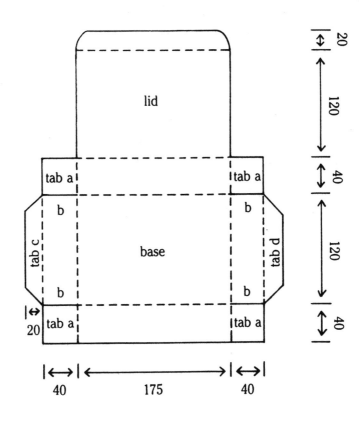

all dimensions in millimetres

13

1.
Preserves, Oils and Vinegars

Tangy vinegars in jewel-bright colours, delicately-flavoured oils, spicy pickles, relishes, chutneys and fruity jams make wonderful seasonal gifts and are especially welcomed by those who do not have the time to make their own.

The flavoured vinegars and oils in this chapter are all suitable for salad dressings. The few included may inspire you to try your own as the variations are endless. Excellent vinegars can be made using the leaves of one of the following: lemon balm, basil, borage, salad burnet, dill, fennel, marjoram, summer savoury, mint, tarragon — which is, perhaps the favourite — or thyme. You can also make a mixed herb vinegar. One good one is made up of summer savoury, marjoram, chives and tarragon, another from basil, rosemary, mint, tarragon and bay. Use good quality red or white wine, cider or sherry vinegar for these. Whatever herbs you use for flavouring should be freshly picked and at their peak. Preferably pick them in the late morning of a hot sunny day; the leaves will be dry and the heat will encourage them to release their fragrance. Herb oils are extremely simple to make and they smell as delicious as they taste. Particularly lovely herb oils can be made using basil, fennel, rosemary, tarragon and thyme. If possible make your herb oils in summer as strong sunlight is needed for the aromatic oils of the herbs to mingle with the oil itself. It is important to choose oils with a light and delicate flavour and light colour; safflower, grapeseed and sunflower are useful and light corn or soya oil may also be used. Olive oil has a very pronounced flavour, but it does go well if using herbs like garlic or mixtures of strong Provence herbs. Experiment with different herbs, using the leaf part only. When you are experimenting just make a small amount and adjust the quantity of herb used for your own personal taste. I guarantee you will get hooked and have a lot of fun experimenting!

Sterilizing jars

Wash jars in hot soapy water and thoroughly rinse them, then stand on a trivet or rack in a large pan of water and bring them to the boil. Remove the jars from the pan, stand upside down to drain, then put into a low oven, 130°C (250°F/Gas Mark ½) to dry.

The jars should be dry and warm (where required). To prevent cracking, stand the jars on a wooden board or on a newspaper and fill to within half an inch of the top, using a small jug, ladle or cup. Wipe the jars immediately, then cover with a waxed disc (waxed side down) and a Cellophane jam cover, or a plastic or plastic-coated screw-top lid, or a special cover for preserves such as Porosan. Label then store preserves in a cool, dry, dark cupboard.

Note: Jars must have plastic or plastic-coated tops to prevent the vinegar corroding the metal. Instant coffee jars, with their plastic lids are particularly useful for pickles and chutneys.

Mixed vegetable pickle

Fills about two 1 pint (600ml) preserving jars

1 Prepare the vegetables: cut the cauliflower into small florets, discarding any leaves and coarse stalks; deseed the pepper, cut into chunks; scrub the carrots, cut into thick slices lengthwise, then cut each slice in half across; top and tail the beans, cut into 1 inch (2.5cm) lengths; slice the cucumber into quarters lengthwise, remove seeds, then cut each quarter in half lengthwise and across; and skin the onions.

2 Layer the vegetables in a large (non-metallic) bowl sprinkling salt between the layers. Pour over 3 pints (1.7 litres) of cold water and cover with a plate to keep the vegetables submerged. Leave in a cool place overnight.

3 Meanwhile put the vinegar and pickling spices in a heatproof bowl and cover with a plate. Set bowl over a saucepan half filled with cold water and bring to the boil. Draw pan (and bowl) off the heat, cover and leave to infuse overnight, then strain.

4 Rinse the vegetables well to remove the salt then pat dry on kitchen paper. Pack them neatly into warm sterilized jars to within 1 inch (2.5cm) of the top of the jar (the vegetables can be layered if wished).

5 Cover the vegetables with cold spiced vinegar to at least ½ inch (1cm) over top layer. Seal with sterilized vinegar-proof lids. Store in a cool, dark place for at least 1 month before opening.

1 medium-sized cauliflower, about 1½ lb (675g) in weight
1 red pepper
2 large carrots weighing about 8 oz (225g)
6 oz (175g) French beans
1 small ridge cucumber about 6 inches (15cm) long
6 oz (175g) small pickling onions
sea salt
3 pints (1.7 litres) cold water
1 pint (600ml) cider vinegar
2 blades mace, 4 allspice berries, a few peppercorns, whole, 1 cinnamon stick and 1 bay leaf for flavouring, or ½ oz (15g) pickling spice

Note
Make sure you get all the air pockets out of the jars (slip a skewer down inside the jars to release them, then turn the jars around a little).

Garlic vinegar

Garlic vinegar is delicious in salad dressings and piquant sauces. The flavour of this vinegar will depend on the freshness of the garlic used.

16 fl oz (450ml) white wine vinegar
5-6 plump cloves of garlic

1 Peel the garlic cloves and leave whole. Thread the cloves on to a bamboo skewer.
2 Place in a sterilized bottle and cover with vinegar. Seal with a vinegar-proof top and leave in a cool, dark place for 2 weeks, shaking occasionally. At the end of 2 weeks, strain and discard cloves if wished.

Note
Take care when peeling the garlic — cuts in the surface will cause the clove to discolour and so spoil the appearance of the vinegar.

Variation
Substitute 4 chopped shallots for garlic.

Pickled onions

1 Cover the onions with boiling water for 1 minute, then drain. This makes them easier to peel.

2 Put the peeled onions in a brine solution — made by dissolving the salt in the cold water. Let the onions soak in the brine for 24 hours. Weight the onions down with a plate, so that they are completely covered by the salt solution.

3 Put the vinegar and mixed pickling spice in a heat-proof bowl and cover with a plate. Set bowl over a saucepan half filled with cold water and bring to the boil. Draw the pan (and bowl) off the heat and leave to infuse for 2 hours, then strain.

4 Drain the onions and rinse them thoroughly under cold running water. Pack the onions tightly into clean jars, allowing ½ inch (1cm) clear space at the top. Push a bay leaf or two in, for flavour and appearance. Any water that settles in the bottom of the jars during packing should be poured off.

5 Pour the cold spiced vinegar over, seal with vinegar-proof lids. Label the jars and store in a cool, dark place for 3 months before using.

4 lb (1.6kg) small pickling onions
4 oz (100g) coarse sea salt
2 pints (1.2 litres) cold water
2 pints (1.2 litres) cider vinegar
1 oz (25g) mixed pickling spice
a few bay leaves

Note
Leave one month if using high-strength (8 per cent) pickling vinegar, or 3 months for ordinary (5 per cent) vinegar.

Pickled walnuts

Fills two 1 lb (450g) jars

As walnuts rarely ripen satisfactorily in Britain, the best way of using the green or unripe walnuts is to pick them in late June or early July whilst they are still soft and 'wet', with outer skin, soft shell and kernel and pickle them whole or use them to make a Walnut-flavoured oil (see page 31).

1 lb (450g) young green walnuts
4 oz (100g) sea salt
2 pints (1.2 litres) water
spiced vinegar, to cover

1 Prick the walnuts all over with a sterilized darning needle so that the brine and pickle can thoroughly penetrate the skins. Discard any walnuts with hard patches at the end opposite to the stalk because this is where the shell starts to form.

2 Place the walnuts in a glass or earthenware bowl (not a metal pan). Dissolve half the salt in half the water, pour this brine over the walnuts. (If the solution does not quite cover the walnuts then make up a little extra, using the same proportion of salt to water.) Cover and leave the walnuts for 5 days in a cool place, stirring twice a day to ensure even brining.

3 Drain off the brine and discard it. Rinse the walnuts in fresh water and return them to the bowl. Make up another brine solution using the remaining water and salt, and any additional brine required, and pour this over the walnuts. Cover and leave for a further week, stirring twice a day as before.

4 Drain, rinse and drain the walnuts again. Spread them out in a single layer on a flat tray or plate. Leave in a sunny place for a couple of days or until the walnuts are completely black.

5 Pack the walnuts into warmed, sterilized jars and cover with spiced vinegar poured over hot. Leave to cool and, when cold, seal the jars with vinegar-proof lids.

6 Label the jars and store them in a cool, dry place for at least six weeks before using.

Note
To help prevent staining your hands, wear fine rubber gloves when handling the walnuts.

Gift wrap
Cut out circles of green and white check gingham to cover the tops of the jars and secure them with narrow white or green ribbon.

Piccalilli

Makes 2 large jars

This is a special type of pickle which is a great favourite with many people because of its spicy mustard sauce. It is delicious with cheese and bread and is useful for sandwiches and to serve with snacks.

1 Chop the courgettes into chunks without peeling them; divide the cauliflower into small florets discarding tough stalks and leaves; top, tail and slice the beans; peel onions and cut in half or quarters if large; peel, remove seeds and dice the marrow.

2 Place the prepared vegetables into a large glass or china bowl. Dissolve the salt in the cold water. Pour this brine over the vegetables, cover with a plate and leave for 24 hours.

3 Tip the vegetables into a colander, rinse thoroughly under cold running water and drain.

4 Mix the sugar, mustard and ginger with 1¾ pints (1 litre) of the vinegar in a large pan. Bring to the boil and simmer gently for 15–20 minutes until the vegetables are just tender. When ready, remove the vegetables with a perforated spoon and pack them into warm, sterilized jars.

5 Blend the flour or cornflour and turmeric to a smooth paste with the remaining vinegar and stir into the vinegar mixture in the pan. Bring to the boil and boil for 3 minutes, stirring continuously. Pour the sauce over the vegetables to within ¼ inch (5mm) of the top. Cover whilst still hot with vinegar-proof lids, and label. Store in a cool, dry place for 4–6 weeks before using.

3¼ lb (1.5kg) prepared vegetables (courgettes, cauliflower, green beans, onions and marrow)
5 oz (150g) coarse sea salt
3½ pints (2 litres) cold water
2 oz (50g) light muscovado or demerara sugar
3 level tablespoons dry mustard
1 level tablespoon ground ginger
2 pints (1.2 litres) white wine vinegar
2 level tablespoons unbleached white flour or cornflour
1 level tablespoon turmeric

Tomato relish

Makes two 1 lb (450g) jars

2 × 16 oz (450g) tins
  chopped tomatoes
1 medium onion, finely
  chopped
1 red pepper, cored, seeded
  and finely chopped
1 green pepper, cored,
  seeded and finely
  chopped
half a large cucumber, peeled
  and chopped
1 clove of garlic, crushed
3 fl oz (75ml) wine or cider
  vinegar
3 tablespoons tomato purée
1 tablespoon mustard seeds
¼–½ teaspoon chilli powder
¼ teaspoon ground coriander
1 teaspoon sea salt
a good pinch of ground
  cumin
1½ tablespoons muscovado
  sugar (optional)

1 Place all the ingredients in a large saucepan and bring slowly to the boil. Simmer, uncovered, for about 30 minutes until most of the liquid has evaporated to give a thick, pulpy consistency. Stir frequently as the relish thickens.
2 Pour into sterilized jars. Seal with sterilized vinegar-proof lids. Label and store in cool, dark place.

Chilli oil

6 small or 3 large fresh
  chillies
16 fl oz (450ml) olive or
  sunflower oil

1 Prick the chillies with a fork or point of a small, sharp knife. Slice large chillies in half lengthways.
2 Take a pretty glass bottle, stoppered with a cork for preference. Drop in the chillies and pour in the oil. Seal the bottle and leave in a sunny place for at least 2 weeks before using. Will keep up to 2 months.

Roasted sweet peppers in oil

Fills a 1 lb (450g) jar

1 Roast the peppers under a high grill or directly over a naked gas flame, turning them over and over until the skin is blackened and blistered all over.
2 Leave them to cool and then peel off the skin, which should come away quite easily if the peppers are well roasted.
3 Cut the peppers in half lengthways and discard the stems and seeds; cut into narrow strips and layer in a sterilized jar with the garlic cloves, sprigs of marjoram and a little sea salt if required.
4 Pour over the oil to cover them completely by ½ inch (1cm) and keep, covered in the refrigerator up to 4 weeks, the flavour maturing with time.

3-4 red peppers
3-4 large cloves of garlic, lightly crushed with a heavy-knife blade and peeled
a few sprigs of fresh marjoram
sea salt (optional)
⅓ pint (200ml) cold pressed olive oil

Gift label
Remove the peppers from the oil and serve in salads, sandwiches, or use in sauces with pasta. Store in the refrigerator, covered with oil, for up to 4 weeks.

Marinated olives

1 Drain off the brine, then rinse the olives in cold water to remove excess salt.
2 Place all the ingredients into an attractive glass jar and cover them completely with olive oil. Seal tightly. Give it a shake to disperse the seeds. Store in a cool, dark place for at least 3 weeks before using.

1 lb (450g) large green olives in brine
2-3 sprigs of thyme
6-8 cloves of garlic, peeled and cut into thick slices
2 tablespoons coriander seeds, bruised
3 small whole dried chillies
olive oil, to cover, preferably extra virgin

Gift label
Serve with drinks as part of a salad selection. The highly-flavoured oil in which the olives have been marinating may be used on its own for cooking or salads.

Pickled aromatic olives

2 lb (900g) large black olives in brine
1 lemon, cut into 12 slices
1 small orange, cut into 12 slices
2 tablespoons cardamom seeds, bruised
2 tablespoons coriander seeds, bruised
olive oil, to cover

1 Drain and rinse the olives under cold running water to remove excess salt.

2 Put a layer of olives in the bottom of a glass jar, add a couple of slices of lemon and orange and a few cardamom and coriander seeds. Keep on layering the olives and the other ingredients until the jar is filled. Slowly pour the olive oil over the olives until they are completely covered. Seal tightly.

3 Store in a cool, dark place for at least 3 weeks before using.

Honey lemon curd

Makes three 12 oz (350g) jars

This is a lemon curd made with honey instead of sugar. It is useful for sweetening desserts, ices, and fruit, or for filling cakes and flans.

4 medium-sized lemons
4 oz (100g) unsalted butter, cut into cubes
1 lb (450g) clear honey
4 free-range eggs
2 extra egg yolks

1 Scrub the lemons; grate their rinds and squeeze out the juice.

2 Place the butter, honey, grated lemon rind and the strained juice in the top of a double saucepan, or in a heatproof bowl over a pan of simmering water.

3 Beat together the eggs and egg yolks and strain on to the other ingredients. Cook, stirring frequently, for 35–40 minutes until the mixture thickens sufficiently to coat the back of a wooden spoon.

4 Pour into warm sterilized jars and cover with waxed discs while hot. When cold, cover with Cellophane discs or lids. Store in the refrigerator. It will keep up to 2 weeks. Use as a filling for flans or spread on wholemeal bread and scones.

Variation
Orange curd. Make as above, but use 3 oranges and 1 lemon.

Gift wrap
Label jars with decorative or coloured labels, then cover tops (over the Cellophane) with pretty fabric cut round the edges with pinking shears. Tie round with fine cord, ribbon or coloured string.

Apricot butter

Fills a 12 oz (350g) jar

1 Wash the apricots well by rinsing them in boiling water, then put them in a saucepan and just cover with water. **2** Bring to the boil, cover and simmer gently for 30 minutes until tender. Drain, reserving the liquid; cool slightly. **3** In a blender or food processor, process the apricots and honey to a purée with a little of the cooking liquid. **4** Spoon into a sterilized jar, seal with a sterilized lid and cool. Store in the refrigerator — allow to mellow for 24 hours before using. You can easily double or triple this recipe.

6 oz (175g) dried apricots
2 tablespoons honey, any kind

Gift label
Store in the refrigerator and eat within 10 days. Use as a filling for cakes or spread on bread or scones.

Bing cherry jam

Makes three 12 oz (350g) jars

2 lb (900g) stoned firm ripe
  cherries
1½ lb (675g) clear honey
1 large juicy lemon (juice and
  pared rind)

1 Place the washed, drained and stoned cherries in a large preserving pan or heavy saucepan with the honey and a large strip of the lemon rind.
2 Bring to a boil over medium heat, stirring constantly. With a slotted spoon, dipped in boiling water and dried, remove the scum from the surface of the jam. Increase the heat and boil rapidly for 20 minutes, stirring to avoid burning until temperature reaches 105°C (221°F), or until setting point is reached. Remove from the heat.
3 Remove and discard the lemon rind and stir in the lemon juice.
4 Ladle the jam into warm sterilized jars to within ¼ inch (5mm) from the top. Seal with sterilized lids. Label and store in a cool, dark place.

Gift wrap
Label jars with decorative labels, then cover tops with fabric cut round the edges with pinking shears. Tie round with fine cord, ribbon or coloured string.

Mushrooms preserved in oil

Fills a 2 pint (1 litre) preserving jar

Small button mushrooms are the most suitable for preserving in oil, as they are usually firm and blemish-free.

1 Wash the mushrooms and trim their stalks, but do not peel. Discard any damaged or blemished ones.
2 In a stainless-steel or enamelled saucepan large enough to take the mushrooms, bring to the boil the vinegar and an equal volume of water. Add the cloves, a pinch of salt, some peppercorns, a bay leaf or two and the mushrooms. Bring back to the boil and simmer for 6–8 minutes, or until the mushrooms are tender but not soft. Drain them thoroughly.
3 Pour a little olive oil in the bottom of a sterilized preserving jar. Put in a layer of mushrooms, a piece of bay leaf, a few peppercorns and half a clove of garlic, cover with oil and continue layering to within ½ inch (1cm) of the top of the jar. The oil must cover the final layer of the mushrooms. Seal and keep in a cool, dark place. The mushrooms will keep for up to six months.

2 lb (900g) button
  mushrooms
1 pint (600ml) white wine
  vinegar
1 pint (600ml) water
6 cloves
salt to taste
1 tablespoon black
  peppercorns
4 bay leaves, halved
olive oil, to cover
3 cloves of garlic, peeled and
  halved

Dried apricot conserve

Makes about 5 lb (2.3kg)

1 lb (450g) dried apricots
3 pints (1.7 litres) cold water
3 tablespoons lemon juice
3 lb (1.4kg) light muscovado
   sugar
2 oz (50g) whole almonds,
   blanched (optional)

1 Wash the apricots under cold running water, then place in a large bowl and cover with the cold water. Leave to soak for 24 hours.

2 Transfer the apricots and soaking liquid to a preserving pan or large saucepan and simmer for 30 minutes or until the apricots are very soft.

3 Add the lemon juice, sugar, and almonds if using, and stir over gentle heat until the sugar is dissolved. Increase the heat and boil rapidly for 5 minutes then test for setting point (see below). If the jam has not set, return the pan to the heat and boil for a further 5 minutes. Repeat until setting point is reached. Remove from the heat. Skim any scum off the surface with a slotted spoon.

4 Allow the jam to stand at room temperature for 15 minutes, stirring occasionally, to keep fruit and nuts in suspension. Ladle into clean, warm, dry jars, and place a waxed paper disc in each jar while the jam is still hot. When cold, seal with Cellophane discs or lids. Store in a cool, dark place.

Gift wrap
Stick attractive labels on the jars, then cover the Cellophane tops with circles of pretty fabric. Tie round with fine cord, ribbon or coloured string. If liked, transport in a small basket lined with tissue paper.

To test for setting point
Spoon a little jam onto a cold plate and draw a finger through the centre. If the mixture stays separate the jam has reached setting point.

Home-made crunchy mustard with honey

1 Put the mustard seeds and vinegar into a bowl, cover and leave for 36 hours.
2 Put the soaked mustard seeds into a blender or food processor with the honey, salt and cinnamon and process until the mixture is thick and creamy. Add a little extra vinegar if the mixture seems too thick.
3 Pot the mixture into small, attractive jars with airtight lids, as otherwise it dries out quickly.

2 oz (50g) white mustard seeds
2 oz (50g) black mustard seeds
¼ pint (150ml) white wine vinegar
3 level teaspoons clear honey
¼ level teaspoon sea salt
¼ level teaspoon ground cinnamon

Gift wrap
Wrap the tops in squares of gingham (or other patterned material), then tie with string. Add a blob of red sealing wax to the knot and a decorative label.

Corn and pepper relish

Makes about 3½ lb (1.75kg)

No selection of pickles and relishes would be complete without a recipe for the ever popular American corn relish.

1 Place the sweetcorn in a pan containing ½ inch (1cm) lightly salted, boiling water. Bring to the boil and boil for 3 minutes. Drain well.
2 Combine the salt, flour, sugar, spices and vinegar in a preserving pan and bring slowly to the boil. Add the onions and peppers to the pan and simmer, uncovered, for 20 minutes or until the vegetables are just tender.
3 Ladle the relish into warm, sterilized jars to within ¼ inch (5mm) of the top. Seal with sterilized vinegar-proof lids. Store in a cool, dark place.

1½ lb (675g) sweetcorn kernels
2 teaspoons sea salt
2 teaspoons unbleached white flour
3 oz (75g) light muscovado sugar
2 teaspoons dry mustard powder
1 teaspoon turmeric
1 tablespoon white mustard seeds
1 pint (600ml) cider or white wine vinegar
2 large onions, peeled and finely chopped
2 red peppers, cored, seeded and finely chopped
2 green peppers, cored, seeded and finely chopped

Gift label
Use as an accompaniment to curries, cheese, or as a filling for sandwiches.

Mushroom ketchup

2 lb (1kg) large, open
   mushrooms
1 oz (25g) sea salt
1 level teaspoon black
   peppercorns
1 level teaspoon whole
   allspice
10 cloves
piece of root ginger
1 pint (600ml) vinegar

1 Cut off bottom of mushroom stalks and discard. Break the mushrooms and stalks in small pieces and place in an earthenware bowl. Sprinkle with the salt, cover and leave to stand for about 12 hours.

2 Place the mushroom mixture in a saucepan and mash with a wooden spoon. Crush the spices in a pestle and mortar and add with the vinegar to the pan. Bring to the boil, cover and simmer for 30 minutes.

3 Pour the mixture into a liquidizer or food processor and blend to make a smooth purée.

4 Pour into hot, sterilized bottles, leaving a 1 inch (2.5cm) headspace, and seal while hot with screw caps.

5 Put a thick wad of newspaper in the bottom of a large deep pan and then stand the filled bottles on this. Fill the pan with hot water reaching up to the bottle necks. Slacken the screw caps by a quarter of a turn and slowly bring the pan of water to the boil and simmer for 30 minutes. Remove the bottles from the water, tighten up the tops, then cool and label. Store in a cool, dry place.

Plum and apple chutney

Fills about 4½ × 1 lb (450g) jars

2 lb (900g) plums (freestone if
   possible)
1 lb (450g) onions
1 lb (450g) seedless raisins
1 lb (450g) cooking apples
   (windfalls are suitable)
1 level tablespoon sea salt
1 teaspoon ground ginger
1 teaspoon ground allspice
¼ teaspoon each of cayenne
   pepper, ground cloves,
   nutmeg and dry mustard
1 pint (600ml) cider vinegar
6 oz (175g) raw cane sugar

1 Wash the plums, cut in half and remove the stones if a freestone variety (if not leave them whole). Peel and chop the onions. Peel, core and chop the apples.

2 Put the plums, onions, raisins and apples in a large saucepan with the salt, spices and half the vinegar. Bring to the boil over high heat, stirring occasionally. Reduce the heat and simmer gently until the contents are soft and pulpy, stirring occasionally. Remove the plum stones if they have not been removed.

3 Add the remaining vinegar and the sugar, bring back to the boil, stirring until the sugar is dissolved and continue simmering until the chutney is thick and with no extra liquid on the surface. Stir occasionally during cooking to prevent sticking.

4 Meanwhile, sterilize the jars: wash and thoroughly rinse them, then stand on a trivet or rack in a large pan of water and bring to the boil. Remove the jars from the pan, stand upside down to drain, then put into a low oven to dry.
5 Remove the pan from the heat. Ladle the chutney into warm, sterilized jars to within ¼ inch (5mm) of top. Cover with waxed paper discs while hot. Seal with sterilized vinegar-proof lids. Cool, label and store in a cool, dry place for up to 6 months.

Note
As an alternative to stoning the plums, count them before cooking. When they are soft, the stones will float free. Remove the right number, crack with a nutcracker and return the kernels to the preserve.

Gift label
Use as an accompaniment to curries, cheese, and savoury pies or as a filling for sandwiches.

Walnut-flavoured oil

Makes 1¾ pints (1 litre)

Walnut oil from France makes a delicious — but expensive — salad dressing. This method using 'wet' or freshly-picked walnuts and a light oil, is an excellent pauper's alternative.

1 Place the oil in a saucepan and warm gently.
2 Remove as much of the thin membrane around the walnuts as possible, then prick each walnut all over.
3 Put the walnuts into a wide-mouth bottle and pour on the oil. Seal tightly. Let stand for 2 weeks, shaking the bottle every 2 or 3 days. Do not strain. Will keep up to 2 months.

1¾ pints (1 litre) safflower or grapeseed oil
8 oz (225g) shelled 'wet' walnuts

Gift label
Store the walnut-flavoured oil in a cool, dark place. Use it as an ingredient in salad dressings or marinades.

Fruity brown sauce

Makes about 3 pints (1.7 litres)

2 lb (900g) cooking apples or windfalls, cored and chopped
12 oz (350g) seedless raisins
½ lb (225g) onions, peeled and sliced
6 oz (175g) cooking dates
2 cloves garlic, peeled and crushed
¾ pint (450ml) spiced vinegar (see page 19)
1 pint (600ml) unsweetened apple juice
1 level teaspoon whole peppercorns
8 whole cloves
½ teaspoon coriander seeds
½ teaspoon ground ginger
½ teaspoon dry mustard
¼ teaspoon cayenne pepper
2 tablespoons miso
1-2 tablespoons tamari (soya sauce)

1 Put all the ingredients except the miso and tamari into a large pan and bring slowly up to the boil. Cover the pan and simmer gently for about an hour, stirring occasionally until very soft.
2 Rub the sauce through a sieve and return to a clean pan. Add the miso and tamari to taste, then bring the sauce back to the boil.
3 Pour into hot bottles leaving a 1 inch (2.5cm) headspace and put on screw tops (not too tightly). Put a thick wad of newspaper in the bottom of a large deep pan and then stand the filled bottles on this. Fill the pan with hot water reaching up to the bottle necks. Bring the water to the boil slowly and simmer for 30 minutes. Seal the caps tightly, cool, label and store in a cool dry place.

Dill vinegar

1 pint (600ml) white wine vinegar
2 tablespoons dill seed

1 Pour the vinegar over the seeds in a wide-mouth bottle. Seal tightly with a vinegar-proof lid, and stand in a dark place for 2 to 3 weeks, shaking it from time to time.
2 Strain the vinegar — using filter paper or cheesecloth — through a funnel into a clean bottle and cork tightly. Use to flavour salads and herb sauces.

Opposite A selection of pickles and preserves (for more ideas see pages 15-36).

Dried Apricot
Conserve

Corn & Pepper
Relish

Mixed Vegetable
Pickle

Rosemary oil

1 Wash rosemary and pat dry. Crush the leaves a little in your fingers to release the aromatic oils. Place in a clean bottle and add the vinegar. Pour in the oil to cover the herbs.
2 Cork the bottle, or put back screw top and leave to marinade on a sunny window-sill for 2–3 weeks, shaking it at least once a day.

2–3 sprigs fresh rosemary
1 teaspoon white wine vinegar
16 fl oz (450ml) olive or sunflower oil

Gift label
Use as you wish, topping up the bottle each time with fresh oil to cover the herbs, until the herb flavour begins to fade.

Rose petal vinegar

Use the petals of the dark-red, old-fashioned damask rose if possible.

1 Wipe rose petals carefully, remove white heel from each petal and place them in a large glass jar.
2 Pour the vinegar over the rose petals, making sure that they are completely covered. Cover and leave the jar on a sunny window-sill to help draw out the flavour for 3–4 weeks.
3 Strain and pour into sterilized bottles. Cover with sterilized corks or plastic screw-top lids. It is ready for use immediately.

3 oz (75g) highly scented rose petals
1¾ pint (1 litre) cider or white wine vinegar

Variations
Violets, primroses, lavender, marigolds, elderflowers, broom flowers and nasturtiums all make excellent vinegars. It is best to use a good white wine for most flowers and a cider vinegar for darker ones like violets or deep-red rose petals.

Opposite A selection of pâtés and savoury spreads (see pages 37-42).

Tarragon vinegar

2 oz (50g) fresh tarragon
1 pint (600ml) white wine
  vinegar
1 fresh sprig tarragon

1 Pack the tarragon into a wide-mouthed jar, bruising the stalks and leaves to bring out the flavour. Fill with vinegar. Seal tightly with a vinegar-proof lid and leave to infuse for 6–8 weeks in a cool, dark place, shaking the jar occasionally.
2 Strain through muslin into a clean bottle and add a fresh sprig of tarragon. Seal tightly with a vinegar-proof lid. Hopefully it will look like those elegant and mysterious bottles in good delicatessens.

Variations
Thyme, marjoram, fennel, sage, salad burnet, lemon balm, rosemary, dill and mint can all be made in the same way as above and used in salad dressings and sauces. Red wine or cider vinegar can be used as a variation.

Note
Pick the tarragon before it flowers and before the full sun has had time to draw out the aromatic oils.

Four herb vinegar

1 sprig rosemary
1 sprig sage
1 sprig thyme
1 sprig tarragon
16 fl oz (450ml) white wine
  or cider vinegar

1 Wash and dry herbs thoroughly. Place in an attractive glass bottle. Pour in the vinegar. Seal with a vinegar-proof lid. Leave to stand, preferably on a sunny window-sill, for 10–14 days. Herbs may be left in the vinegar while it is being used, or removed.

Aromatic oil

1¾ pints (1 litre) olive oil,
  preferably cold-pressed
  extra virgin
3 sprigs rosemary
6 sprigs thyme
1 large clove garlic
1 green chilli pepper
5 small red chilli peppers
8 black peppercorns
6 juniper berries

1 Pour the oil into an attractive glass bottle (stoppered with a cork for preference).
2 Wash the herbs and pat them dry on kitchen paper. Peel and halve the garlic. Prick the chillies with a fork or point of a small, sharp knife.
3 Drop the herbs into the bottle, with the garlic, chilli peppers, peppercorns and juniper berries. Seal tightly. Keep for 2 weeks before using. Do not strain. It looks particularly pretty with the herbs floating in it.

The cork can be sealed with red sealing wax. Dip the neck of the bottle into the melted wax until about 1 inch (2.5cm) of the neck is fully immersed. Lift away the bottle and give it a slight twist to shed excess liquid wax.

Gift wrap
Wrap in sacking or hessian and tie round the top with string.

Raspberry-flavoured vinegar

1 Place the vinegar and 8 oz (225g) raspberries in a glass or china bowl and crush the raspberries well with a wooden spoon to allow the juice to start flowing. Cover the bowl with a clean cloth or a piece of cling-film and leave to stand for 3 days in a cool, dark place, giving an occasional stir.

2 Strain the vinegar through a fine nylon sieve into a clean bowl. Discard the raspberries and repeat the process by pouring the strained vinegar over the second batch of crushed fruit and letting it stand for 3 days as before.

3 Strain and decant into clean sterilized bottles with a few whole fruit in the base. Seal with vinegar-proof screw-top lids or corks. Store in a cool, dark place until needed.

1 pint (600ml) white wine vinegar
2×8 oz (225g) fresh raspberries (purchased in separate lots, 3 days apart)

Variations
Blackberries, wineberries or blackcurrants prepared in the same way make excellent fruit vinegars, too.

Gift wrap
Attach a decorative label to the bottle, describing contents, then wrap in fancy paper as though you were wrapping a wine bottle.

Kumquat marmalade

Makes 2×8 oz (225g) jars

1 lb (450g) kumquats
7 fl oz (200ml) apple and
    orange juice concentrate

1 Sterilize two 8 oz (225g) jars and place in a very cool oven, 130°C (250°F/Gas Mark ½) to keep warm until needed.
2 Scrub the kumquats well, cut in half and remove pips. Process with the concentrated apple and orange juice in a liquidizer or food processor until the kumquats are quite small.
3 Place the mixture in a saucepan and bring to the boil. After 15 minutes test with the plate test to see if it is set (see below).
4 Pour to within ½ inch (1cm) of the top of the sterilized jars, cover; seal tightly with sterilized lids. Store in the refrigerator.

Plate test
Pour a small amount of marmalade on to a cold plate. Let stand until cold. If the mixture stays separate when a finger is drawn through the centre, the marmalade has reached setting point. Remove the marmalade from the heat while test marmalade is cooling.

Gift label
Store in the refrigerator. It will keep for up to six weeks after opening.

2.
Pâtés and Savoury Spreads

Pack them in small pots or jars, in foil containers or small plastic cups — unless you want to make a small china terrine or pottery dish part of the present. Soup bowls with lids make ideal pâté containers while small glass tumblers are perfect for giving nut butters and spreads.

If you want to give a selection of nut butters, say American Style Peanut Butter, Cashew Butter and Almond butter try to use jars of similar shapes and sizes, then follow that up by packaging them all in the same way — similar labels, and matching cover material and ribbons on all three. This will give a unity to the gift and they can be presented together in a box.

Mushroom and olive pâté

Makes about 1½ lb (675g)

6 tablespoons olive oil
1 large onion, finely chopped
2 large cloves garlic, peeled and crushed
12 oz (350g) large open cap mushrooms, roughly chopped
8 oz (225g) stoned black olives, chopped
1 teaspoon mixed herbs
Sea salt and freshly ground black pepper
2 oz (50g) walnut pieces
clarified butter, to cover (see below)

1 Heat the oil in a pan, add the onion and garlic and fry until the onion is transparent. Add the mushrooms, olives and herbs and cook, stirring, until all the liquid has evaporated and the mushrooms are tender. Season with salt and pepper.
2 Blend the cooked mixture with the walnut pieces to a rough purée in a food processor.
3 Spoon the pâté into a small pottery dish with a lid or a soufflé dish and smooth the top down with the back of a spoon. Leave ½ inch (1cm) headspace. Cover with about ⅛ inch (3mm) clarified butter. Store in the refrigerator. This will keep for up to 2 weeks if the butter seal is left undisturbed.

Note
Clarify the butter by placing it in a heavy-based saucepan over a low heat. Leave until it is foaming slightly. Pour the melted butter through a sieve lined with butter muslin or cheesecloth, leaving the whitish residue behind. As a guide, 8 oz (225g) of unclarified butter will make approximately 6 oz (175g) of clarified butter.

Gift wrap
Seal lid to dish with Sellotape, then pack into a box. Wrap in suitable paper, then tie with ribbon, string or braid.

Potted Stilton

A good Christmas present for Stilton lovers.

8 oz (225g) fresh Stilton cheese
3 oz (75g) unsalted butter
a pinch ground mace
1 dessertspoon ruby or vintage port
a little melted clarified butter, to run over the top (see Mushroom and olive pâté, above)

1 Trim away the rind and break the Stilton into a mixing bowl. Mash very thoroughly with a fork.
2 Soften the butter and add to the cheese together with the ground mace. Blend together well. Gradually beat in the port.
3 Pack the mixture into small earthenware or pottery pots, (ramekin dishes are fine), tapping them on the table while filling to knock out any air-holes. Leave ½ inch (1cm) headspace.

4 Smooth over the tops and cover with about ⅛ inch (3mm) clarified butter. Cover with transparent film and keep in the refrigerator for up to 2 weeks.

Gift label
Allow the cheese to come to room temperature before serving. Accompany with Melba toast, biscuits or crackers.
.

Almond butter

1 Spread whole, blanched almonds in a single layer on a large baking sheet. Place in a preheated moderate oven, 180°C (350°F/Gas Mark 4), for about 10-15 minutes. Shake and stir frequently. Remove from the oven when the almonds are an even, pale golden colour. Leave to cool.
2 Grind the almonds in a blender or food processor, adding oil as necessary to form a spreadable paste. Add salt to taste. Pack into clean jars and seal. Store in the refrigerator. This spread will keep for about 2 months.

12 oz (350g) whole almonds, blanched (see below)
3-4 tablespoons sunflower oil
¼ teaspoon sea salt (optional)

Note
To blanch the almonds: place the nuts in a small bowl and cover with boiling water. Leave for 3 minutes. Remove, one at a time with a spoon, and press between the thumb and the forefinger. The skin should slip off easily. Dry the nuts on a cloth. If the almonds are not to be used immediately, put them on a rack in a very cool oven, 110°C (225°F/Gas Mark ¼) for 2 hours to dry. Store in an airtight container.

Gift wrap
Pack the almond butter into a small pottery mug with a handle. Cover with cling-film and attach a card to the handle with ribbon or thick thread.

Hazelnut spread

1 lb (450g) shelled hazelnuts
2-3 tablespoons sunflower
  oil, or more as needed
¼ teaspoon sea salt
  (optional)

1 Spread the hazelnuts in a single layer on a baking sheet and place under a preheated moderate grill until the skins split, shaking frequently. Turn into a rough towel and rub off the loose skins. Leave the nuts to cool.

2 Grind the hazelnuts in a blender or food processor, adding oil as necessary, to make a nut butter of smooth consistency. Season with salt to taste. Pack into clean screw-top jars and seal. Store in the refrigerator for up to 2 months.

Gift wrap
As for Almond Butter (see page 39).

American-style peanut butter

2 tablespoons apple juice
  concentrate
1 lb (450g) unsalted roasted
  peanuts
approximately 6 tablespoons
  ground nut or soya oil
½ level teaspoon sea salt
  (optional)

1 Place the apple juice concentrate and half the peanuts into an electric blender or food processor and blend on medium speed gradually adding the oil. Process until the mixture is smooth and thick.

2 Add the remainder of the peanuts and the salt (if using), blend a few seconds more for a crunchy peanut butter or longer for smooth peanut butter — according to which you prefer. A little extra oil may be needed, depending on how quickly the peanuts absorb the oil.

3 Pack into clean screw-top jars and cover. Store in the refrigerator for up to 2 months.

Note
Do not use dry-roasted peanuts.

Kalamata olive pâté

Makes 12 oz (350g)

1 Place all the ingredients in a blender or food processor and blend until smooth. If using a blender, the machine will have to be stopped frequently and a plastic spatula used to push the mixture onto the blender blades repeatedly until a smooth paste is obtained.
2 Pot in tightly covered glass jars and label with date.

1 lb (450g) Kalamata olives (Greek olives preserved in brine and olive oil) pitted
1 large clove garlic, peeled
2 teaspoons mixed herbs
1-2 tablespoons brandy (optional)
3-4 tablespoons olive oil, preferably extra-virgin

Gift label
An aromatic black olive spread. Delicious on toast, accompanied by tomato, hard-boiled egg, or cheese. May also be used with pasta, quiche, salads and jacket potatoes. Store in the refrigerator, use within one month.

Potted cheese with walnuts

1 Mix the cheeses with the butter and mustard. Gradually stir in the sherry until a very firm paste is formed (the amount of sherry depends on the dryness of the cheese).
2 Stir in the walnuts and pack firmly into a soufflé dish or earthenware pot and top with walnut halves. Cover and chill. Store in the refrigerator until required (up to 3 days).

4 oz (100g) Stilton cheese, crumbled
4 oz (100g) Cheddar cheese, grated
3 oz (75g) unsalted butter, softened
1 level teaspoon French mustard
1-2 tablespoons medium-dry sherry
2-3 oz (50-75g) walnuts, roughly chopped
walnut halves, to garnish

Gift label
Accompany with fresh vegetables and wholemeal biscuits. Serves 6-8.

Cashew butter

Makes 2 × 12 oz (350g) jars

1 lb (450g) cashew pieces
6 tablespoons sunflower oil
(approximately)
¼ level teaspoon sea salt
(optional)

1 Spread the cashew pieces in a single layer on a baking sheet. Place in the top of a preheated moderate oven, 180°C, (350°F/Gas Mark 4), for about 10 minutes until pale gold, turning them or shaking the tray from time to time. Leave them to cool.

2 Grind the cashews in a blender or food processor, adding oil as necessary to make a nut butter of smooth consistency. Add salt to taste if using.

3 Spoon into sterilized jars and seal. Alternatively, pack into glass tumblers and cover tops with non-PVC cling-film. Store in the refrigerator for up to 2 months.

Gift wrap
As for Almond Butter (see page 39).

3.
Savoury Cocktail Nibbles

Cocktail biscuits and spiced nuts are always useful as small gifts to take to family and friends when visiting or to have with drinks. They can be given in plastic bags, which make carrying easy and eliminate breakage of storage jars *en route* to the recipient. However, they do look best in glass storage jars or family-sized instant coffee jars (give a coat of enamel paint to eradicate any lettering on the lid). The important thing is that the containers should be airtight.

Devilled mixed nuts

1½ oz (40g) unsalted butter
1 clove garlic, peeled and
  crushed
1 teaspoon vegetarian
  Worcestershire sauce
1 teaspoon curry powder
a good pinch cayenne pepper
4 oz (100g) each whole
  blanched almonds, raw
  cashew nuts and pecan
  halves

1 In a medium saucepan, melt the butter over low heat. Add the garlic, Worcestershire sauce, curry powder and cayenne pepper. Remove from the heat and add the nuts, stir well to coat evenly with the spicy butter mixture.
2 Place the nuts in an ovenproof dish and bake in a preheated moderate oven, 180°C, (350°F/Gas Mark 4) for 15–20 minutes, stirring every 5 minutes to ensure even browning. Remove the nuts from the oven and allow to cool completely before storing in an airtight container.

Gift wrap
Pack the nuts into a screw-top glass jar and decorate with a bow made of coloured ribbon, or use small wooden bowls and give as part of the present.

Garlic almonds

½ oz (15g) unsalted butter
3 large cloves garlic, peeled
6 oz (175g) blanched
  almonds
sea salt, to taste

1 Melt the butter in a shallow ovenproof dish in a preheated moderate oven, 190°C (375°F/Gas Mark 5). Crush the garlic, add to the butter and return to the oven for 3 minutes.
2 Add the almonds and roast for 12–15 minutes until golden brown. Turn occasionally during cooking to ensure even roasting.
3 Spread the nuts on crumpled kitchen paper to remove excess butter then sprinkle with salt to taste.
4 Cool, then pack into an airtight container.

Gift wrap
Pack the nuts into a screw-top glass jar. Alternatively, pack into a small pottery mug with handle. Cover with cling-film. Attach a card to the handle with ribbon or thick thread for a more costly present.

Spiced cashews

1 Heat the butter in a large frying pan. Add the nuts and spices and cook over a medium heat, stirring almost constantly, for 10–15 minutes or until nuts are toasted.
2 Spread nuts on a baking sheet. Cool completely, then pack into an airtight container.

1 oz (25g) unsalted butter
12 oz (350g) raw whole cashews
½ teaspoon ground cinnamon
½ teaspoon ground allspice

Gift wrap
As for Devilled Mixed Nuts (see page 44).

Tropical trail mix

1 Mix together all the ingredients and transfer to a glass jar with stopper. Store for up to 3 weeks.

6 oz (175g) seedless raisins
4 oz (100g) banana chips
4 oz (100g) dried apricots, chopped
4 oz (100g) sunflower seeds
2 oz (50g) toasted coconut flakes
2 oz (50g) glacé pineapple, chopped

Gift wrap
Wrap in fancy gift paper and tie round with ribbon or braid.

Curried pumpkin seeds

Makes 1 small bowlful

1 Place the garlic, curry powder and salt into a small saucepan with the warm water. Mix well, add the cold water and heat to simmering point.
2 Remove from the heat and add the pumpkin seeds. Stir and mix well. Allow the pumpkin seeds to soak in the mixture for 5 minutes, stirring from time to time.
3 Spread the seeds on a baking sheet and dot with butter. Sprinkle with salt to taste. Toast in a preheated cool oven, 150°C (300°F/Gas Mark 2), for 15–20 minutes, or until crisp.
4 Cool and store in a screw-top jar.

1 clove garlic, peeled and crushed
1½ tablespoons curry powder
½ teaspoon sea salt
2 tablespoons warm water
3 fl oz (75ml) cold water
6 oz (175g) unsalted pumpkin seeds
1 teaspoon unsalted butter
sea salt, for sprinkling

Gift wrap
As for Devilled Mixed Nuts (see page 44).

Cocktail cheese fancies

Mouthwatering savoury biscuits, ideal to serve with drinks. Makes about 40.

6 oz (175g) fine plain wholemeal pastry flour
pinch sea salt
3 oz (75g) unsalted butter or soft vegetable margarine
2 oz (50g) mature Cheddar cheese, finely grated
a good pinch cayenne pepper
¼ teaspoon mustard powder
free-range egg yolk
2-3 teaspoons cold water
milk, for glazing
grated Parmesan cheese, paprika pepper, poppy seeds, sesame seeds or caraway seeds, to decorate

1 Place the flour and salt in a bowl and rub in the butter or margarine until the mixture resembles fine breadcrumbs. Stir in the grated cheese, cayenne pepper and mustard powder. Add the egg yolk and enough water to make a soft dough.
2 Knead the pastry lightly then roll out to a scant ¼ inch (5mm) thickness. Cut into a selection of shapes, i.e., squares, diamonds or triangles, or stamp into rounds with a 1½ inch (4cm) plain biscuit cutter.
3 Place the biscuits on ungreased baking sheets. Brush with milk and sprinkle with Parmesan cheese, paprika pepper, poppy seeds, sesame seeds or caraway seeds.
4 Bake in a preheated moderately hot oven, 200°C (400°F/Gas Mark 6), for about 10 minutes or until light golden brown. Transfer to a wire rack and allow to cool and crisp up. Store in an airtight container until needed.

Note
The biscuits will stay fresh if kept in an airtight container for 10 days — alternatively freeze the uncooked biscuits, ready cut, and then bake straight from frozen when needed.

Gift wrap
Arrange a selection of these shaped biscuits in an attractive airtight tin to give as a 'second' present.

Shoyu roasted seeds

1 Mix all the ingredients together in a bowl. Leave aside for 15 minutes.
2 Spread the sunflower and pumpkin seeds on a lightly-oiled baking sheet and roast in a preheated moderate oven, 190°C (375°F/Gas Mark 5), for 10–15 minutes. Turn occasionally during cooking to ensure even roasting. Cool and store in a screw-top jar.

4 oz (100g) sunflower seeds
4 oz (100g) pumpkin seeds
2 tablespoons shoyu soya sauce

Gift wrap
As for Devilled Mixed Nuts (see page 44).

Home salted nuts

Almonds, brazils or cashews can all be prepared like this and make a delicious present.

1 Heat the butter and oil in a frying pan, add the nuts and fry over moderate heat, turning constantly until they are evenly golden brown.
2 Remove from the pan with a slotted spoon and drain on crumpled kitchen paper. Toss, while still hot, with salt to taste.
3 Cool, then pack into an airtight container.

1 oz (25g) unsalted butter
1 teaspoon sunflower or vegetable oil
4 oz (100g) blanched almonds, cashew nuts, Brazil nuts or walnuts
a little sea salt

Gift wrap
Pack in small wooden bowls and give as part of the present, or use small Cellophane see-through bags with labels.

Pretzels

Makes 36 pretzels

2 teaspoons dried yeast
¼ pint (150ml) warm water
4 teaspoons clear honey
½ oz (15g) unsalted butter
sea salt
¼ pint (150ml) milk
1 lb (450g) strong wholemeal
    flour
1 egg white
coarse sea salt, poppy seeds,
    or sesame seeds, to
    decorate

1 In a small bowl, mix together the yeast, warm water and 1 teaspoon of honey. Set aside and allow the yeast to become foamy.

2 In a saucepan, combine the butter, remaining 3 teaspoons of honey, 1 teaspoon salt and milk. Heat gently until the butter and honey melt. Pour liquid into a large warmed bowl. Add the yeast, then beat the flour into the yeast mixture until the dough cleans the sides of the bowl.

3 Turn onto floured surface and knead for 8–10 minutes until smooth and elastic. Place in a clean bowl, cover with a damp cloth and leave to rise in a warm place for about 1 hour, until doubled in size.

4 Turn onto a floured surface, knead for a few minutes, then divide into 4 portions. Set aside 3 portions. Divide the remaining portion into 9 small pieces. Roll each piece into a 'rope' about the thickness of a pencil and 12 inches (30cm) long.

5 Shape each rope into a circle, overlapping about 4 inches (10cm) from each end, leaving the ends free. Take one end of dough in each hand and twist at the point where the dough overlaps (see diagram). Carefully lift ends across to the opposite edges of the circle. Tuck ends under edge for pretzel shape, moisten and press lightly to seal. Repeat with the remaining dough.

6 Place the pretzels on lightly-greased baking sheets and leave to prove until just beginning to rise — about 10 minutes.

7 Bring a large pan of water to the boil with 2 tablespoons of salt. Carefully drop the pretzels, a few at a time, into the water and boil for 2 minutes, turning once. Remove from the water with a slotted spoon. Drain for a few minutes on a wire rack. Place ½ inch (1cm) apart on greased baking sheets. Brush with egg white mixed with water. Sprinkle with poppy seeds, sesame seeds or coarse sea salt.

8 Bake in a preheated very hot oven, 230°C (450°F/Gas Mark 8), for 20-25 minutes, or until golden brown. Transfer the pretzels to a wire rack to cool.

Form dough rope into a circle with overlapping ends, twist the ends and fold back into the circle and secure.

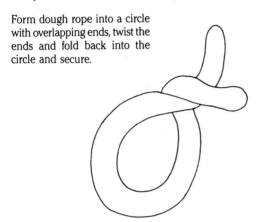

Finished pretzel shape

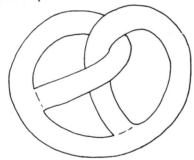

4.
Biscuits

Home-made biscuits are ideal to give as presents or to sell at fund-raising activities. Here I have included ideas that will appeal to every age, from alphabet biscuits for the very young, to traditional favourites like gingerbread men, brandy snaps, and even edible gift labels!

Biscuits are easy to make and with the help of cutters you can turn out a big range of shapes which will rival any bought assortment. Most biscuits keep several weeks if stored in airtight containers.

They make a gift on their own, packed into a decorative cardboard box lined with lace paper doilies, in a plastic bag tied with a pretty ribbon or in any large necked jar or container. The biscuits can also be stacked, close wrapped in cling-film and then wrapped in tissue or crêpe paper to look like a party cracker.

Two general tips:
Don't try to make your biscuits too thin, as they will tend to be harder and don't bake them too long — remember they will crisp up as they cool.

Biscuit alphabet

For the first time, having to eat your words can be fun
— and tasty! Spelling birthday and holiday greetings and
making edible valentines are the most obvious uses, but
others will no doubt come to mind.

1 Put the butter, sugar and honey into a small saucepan
and heat gently until the butter has melted and the sugar
dissolved. Cool slightly, then stir in the cream.
2 Sift the flour, spices and baking powder into a bowl,
and add the bran left in the sieve. Make a well in the centre
and stir in the melted ingredients. Mix together well to
form a dough. Wrap and chill for at least 30 minutes.
3 Knead the dough on a lightly-floured surface then roll
out to ¼ inch (5mm) thickness. Using alphabet cutters
stamp out the biscuits, rerolling the dough as necessary.
Alternatively, roll dough between hands and shape into
letters.
4 Place the biscuits on lightly-oiled baking sheets and
bake in a preheated hot oven, 220°C (425°F/Gas Mark
7), for about 10 minutes. Transfer to a wire rack to cool.
5 Store in an airtight tin until ready for packing.

2 oz (50g) unsalted butter or
   soft vegetable margarine
2 oz (50g) demerara sugar
2 fl oz (50ml) clear honey
4 tablespoons single cream
8 oz (225g) fine wholemeal
   pastry flour
½ teaspoon ground
   cinnamon
¼ teaspoon ground cloves
¼ teaspoon ground nutmeg
¾ teaspoon ground ginger
1 teaspoon baking powder

Note
The dough seems very soft when it is first prepared but it firms up
as it is chilled.

Gift wrap
Pack carefully in a tissue-lined box with the letters forming a secret
message for the recipient to unscramble.

Date and oat slices

Makes 16

8 oz (225g) wholemeal flour
4 oz (100g) rolled oats
3 oz (75g) demerara sugar
5 oz (150g) unsalted butter or
　　soft vegetable margarine

Filling:
12 oz (350g) chopped dates
6 tablespoons water
grated rind ½ lemon or
　　orange

1 Put the filling ingredients in a medium-sized pan and simmer gently until the dates are soft and pulpy.
2 Mix together the flour, oats and sugar. Melt the butter or margarine over a low heat and stir in the dry ingredients, combining everything thoroughly.
3 Spread half the oat mixture into an 11 × 7 inch (27 × 18cm) shallow baking tin, pressing down firmly. Cover with the dates and sprinkle the remaining oat mixture over and press down well.
4 Bake in a preheated moderately hot oven, 190°C (375°F/Gas Mark 5), for 25–30 minutes, until golden brown. Cut into slices while warm, then cool completely in the tin before removing carefully.

Variations
Substitute dried apricots or figs for the dates.

Gift wrap
As for Almond Slices (see page 71).

Carob chip cookies

Makes 30

1 Cream the butter or margarine with the honey until light and fluffy. Gradually beat in the egg. Stir in the remaining ingredients and mix well.
2 Place small spoonfuls of the mixture on a lightly-oiled baking sheet, well apart. Bake in a preheated moderate oven 190°C (375°F/Gas Mark 5), for 15 minutes until golden. Transfer to a wire cooling-rack where they will crisp up as they cool. Store in an airtight tin.

4 oz (100g) unsalted butter or soft vegetable margarine
5 tablespoons clear honey
1 free-range egg, beaten
6 oz (175g) 100 percent self-raising wholemeal flour, sifted
4 oz (100g) no-added-sugar plain carob bar, chopped
2 oz (50g) chopped walnuts

Gift wrap
Place in a plastic bag and tie with a ribbon or pack into a glass cookie jar.

Scottish shortbread

Makes 8 biscuits

5 oz (150g) 100 percent fine
milled wholemeal flour
1 oz (25g) brown rice flour
1 oz (25g) molasses sugar
4 oz (100g) unsalted butter or
polyunsaturated
margarine

1 Mix the flours into a bowl and stir in the sugar. Rub the butter into the dry ingredients until the mixture begins to stick together, then press lightly to form a soft dough. Knead carefully on a lightly-floured surface until fairly smooth.

2 Press the dough into a 7-inch (18cm) round sandwich tin with the back of a metal spoon and level the surface. Mark the top of the dough all over with a fork and crimp the edges. Alternatively, press the mixture into a lightly-floured 7-inch (18cm) round shortbread mould. Then carefully turn it out on to a lightly-oiled baking sheet.

3 Bake the shortbread in a preheated cool oven, 150°C (300°F/Gas Mark 2), for 45 minutes, or until it is just coloured. Retrace the markings and leave to cool in the tin. Remove and store in an airtight tin. Will keep fresh for up to 10 days.

Gift wrap
Pack into a doily-lined 7-inch (18cm) round shallow wicker basket. Wrap with clear Cellophane paper, then tie round with ribbon — tartan if you can find it. Alternatively, present the shortbread round with the traditional wooden mould used to make it, along with a copy of the recipe.

Apricot and date flapjacks

Makes 10

1 Melt the margarine with the honey and sugar in a pan. Stir in the oats, apricots, dates and cinnamon and mix thoroughly. Turn into a lightly-oiled shallow 8 inch (20cm) square tin and smooth the top with a palette knife.
2 Bake in a preheated moderate oven, 180°C (350°F/Gas Mark 4), for 25-30 minutes until golden brown.
3 Cool in the tin for 2 minutes, then cut into fingers. Cool completely before removing from the tin.

5 oz (150g) soft vegetable margarine
4 tablespoons clear honey
2 oz (50g) muscovado sugar
4 oz (100g) rolled oats
4 oz (100g) jumbo oats
3 oz (75g) dried apricots, finely chopped
3 oz (75g) pitted dates, chopped
½ teaspoon ground cinnamon

Gift wrap
Pack into a doily-lined tin with well-fitting lid, or a basket. If using a basket, wrap securely with Cellophane to keep the biscuits crisp.

Christmas tree biscuits

Makes about 16 biscuits

1 Cream the butter and sugar together until light and fluffy. Beat in the egg with 1 tablespoon of the flour. Mix in the remaining flour with the baking powder and the chopped nuts, to give a firm dough.
2 Turn the dough onto a lightly-floured surface and knead until smooth (knead in a little more flour if the mixture is too sticky to roll out). Roll out to ¼ inch (5mm) thick. Stamp out the biscuits with a Christmas tree cutter about 5 inches (12.5cm) long, re-rolling and re-cutting the trimmings.
3 Place the biscuits on a lightly-oiled baking sheet. Press split almonds on the edge of the tree leaves and half a walnut at the base to represent the trunk of the tree.
4 Bake in a preheated moderate oven, 180°C (350°F/Gas Mark 4), for 15-20 minutes or until the biscuits and almonds are lightly browned. Leave to cool for 2 minutes then transfer to a wire rack to cool completely. Store in an airtight tin until required.

4 oz (100g) unsalted butter, softened
3 oz (75g) light muscovado sugar
1 free-range egg, beaten
8oz (225g) fine wholemeal flour
1 teaspoon baking powder
4 oz (100g) mixed chopped nuts
split almonds and walnut halves, for decoration

Gift wrap
Pack carefully in a doily-lined box in layers, with tissue paper between.

Brandy snaps

Makes about 20

2 oz (50g) unsalted butter or
polyunsaturated
margarine
2 oz (50g) honey
2 oz (50g) raw demerara
sugar
2 oz (50g) 100 percent
wholemeal flour
½ teaspoon ground ginger
1 teaspoon brandy

1 Heat the butter or margarine, honey and sugar in a saucepan, stirring occasionally until the margarine has melted. Remove from the heat and stir in the remaining ingredients until well blended.

2 Drop teaspoonfuls of the mixture about 2 inches (5cm) apart on a lightly-oiled baking sheet. Bake in a preheated moderate oven 160°C (325°F/Gas Mark 3), for 8–10 minutes until golden brown.

3 Remove from the oven, allow to cool slightly then loosen the brandy snaps with a palette knife. Roll each snap smooth side outwards around the handle of a wooden spoon, slip off and follow quickly with the next. If the snaps harden before you have time to roll them, return them to the oven for a few seconds. Repeat with the remaining snaps. Cool completely on a wire rack. Store in an airtight container for up to 10 days.

Variation
Sesame seed snaps. Add 2 tablespoons of sesame seeds to the basic mixture. Bake as above. Mould around a rolling pin.

Note
Make these biscuits in small batches, so that they do not have time to cool and become brittle before they are shaped.

Gift label
Serve plain or filled with whipped cream or thick Greek-style yogurt.

Carob digestive biscuits

Makes about 12

1 Mix the flour, oatmeal and baking powder together. Rub in the margarine until the mixture resembles breadcrumbs. Stir in the sugar and add enough milk to make a soft manageable dough. Knead lightly.

2 Roll out on a lightly-floured board to a thickness of about ¼ inch (5mm). Using a 3 inch (7.5cm) plain round biscuit cutter stamp out the biscuits. Prick all over with a fork and transfer them to a greased baking sheet.

3 Bake in a preheated moderate oven, 180°C (350°F/Gas Mark 4), for 15–20 minutes, until light brown. Transfer to a wire rack to cool.

4 When cold, melt the carob in the top of a double boiler or in a bowl over a pan of hot water. Stir in the milk. Using a palette knife, spread the top of the biscuits with the melted carob. Just before it sets make patterns in the carob with a fork. Allow the carob to cool completely before storing the biscuits in an airtight tin.

6 oz (175g) 100 percent wholemeal flour
2 oz (50g) medium oatmeal
1 teaspoon baking powder
3 oz (75g) unsalted butter or soft vegetable margarine
1½ oz (40g) light muscovado sugar
3–4 tablespoons skimmed milk, to mix
4 oz (100g) plain no-added-sugar carob bar, broken into pieces
1 tablespoon skimmed milk

Gift wrap
Pack into a box or tin, wrap with fancy paper and tie with ribbon.

Peanut butter cookies

Makes about 24

Use an unsweetened peanut butter made only from roasted peanuts and salt.

4 fl oz (100ml) corn germ oil
4 fl oz (100ml) clear honey
6 oz (175g) crunchy peanut
  butter
1 large free-range egg
4 oz (100g) porridge oats
8 oz (225g) wholemeal flour
2 oz (50g) desiccated coconut
  (unsweetened)

1 In a large bowl, combine the oil, honey, peanut butter and egg until well blended. Add the dry ingredients and mix thoroughly.
2 Place tablespoonsful of the mixture, spaced well apart, onto greased baking sheets. Press each one down slightly with the back of a fork. Bake in a preheated moderate oven, 180°C (350°F/Gas Mark 4), for 15–20 minutes. Cool on a wire rack and store in a tin when cold.

Gift wrap
Pack in a stoneware jar with cork stopper, or in a glass storage jar with a well-fitting lid. Tie round with ribbon.

Star cookies

Makes 9

1 Cream the butter or margarine with the sugar until light and fluffy. Beat in the egg. Sift in the flour, cinnamon and ground almonds, adding the bran left in the sieve. Fold the dry ingredients in with a metal spoon and knead the mixture lightly to produce a smooth, soft dough.

2 Roll the dough out on a lightly-floured surface until ⅛ inch (3mm) thick and stamp out the biscuits with a 3-inch (7.5cm) star cutter, re-rolling and re-cutting the trimmings to give the required number of biscuits. With a ¾-inch (2cm) plain round cutter, stamp out the centre from half the stars.

3 Arrange the biscuits on greased baking sheets and bake in a preheated moderate oven, 180°C (350°F/Gas Mark 4), for 15–20 minutes, until golden brown. Lift on to wire racks and leave them to cool.

4 Spread the cookies without a hole with strawberry jam. Pair with the remainder. Fill the holes with a little more jam, if necessary. Store in an airtight container until required.

2 oz (50g) unsalted butter or soft vegetable margarine
2 oz (50g) muscovado sugar
1 free-range egg
5 oz (150g) wholemeal flour
1 teaspoon ground cinnamon
1½ oz (40g) ground almonds
3-4 tablespoons no-added-sugar strawberry jam

Variation
For a St Valentine's Day gift use heart-shaped biscuit cutters instead of stars.

Note
With jam the cookies will keep in an airtight tin for 3–4 days, without jam for up to one week.

Gift wrap
Using cling-film, wrap the cookies together in groups of three then tie each package with a narrow red ribbon.

Easter biscuits

Makes about 12

3 oz (75g) unsalted butter or soft vegetable margarine
3 oz (75g) light muscovado sugar
1 free-range egg, separated
6 oz (175g) fine plain wholemeal pastry flour
½ teaspoon baking powder
½ teaspoon mixed spice
½ teaspoon ground cinnamon
2 oz (50g) currants
grated rind ½ lemon
2-3 tablespoons cold milk, to mix

1 Cream the butter or margarine with the sugar until light and fluffy. Beat in the egg yolk. Sieve in the flour, baking powder and spices and add the bran left in the sieve. Add the currants and grated lemon rind and enough milk to make the mixture hold together yet still keep firm — it should not need much. Refrigerate for 15 minutes.

2 Turn the dough onto a lightly-floured surface, roll out to an ⅛ inch (3mm) thickness and stamp out rounds with a 3-inch (7.5cm) fluted cutter, rerolling and recutting the trimmings to give the required number of biscuits.

3 Put the rounds on to two lightly-oiled baking sheets, leaving room for the biscuits to spread. Lightly whisk the egg-white and glaze the biscuits.

4 Bake at the top and centre of a preheated moderate oven, 180°C (350°F/Gas Mark 4), for 12–15 minutes until golden. Transfer to a wire rack, leave to cool, then store in an airtight tin until ready for packing.

Gift wrap
Pack carefully in a doily-lined box in layers with tissue paper between. Cover with lid if it fits, or wrap with coloured Cellophane paper. If liked, decorate with a couple of Easter chicks.

Gingerbread men

Makes about 12

The number of biscuits that can be made with this recipe depends on the size of the biscuit cutters used. These look very festive tied to the Christmas tree with bright green or red ribbon.

1 In a large bowl, combine the oil, water, honey and molasses or treacle. Stir in the salt, bicarbonate of soda and spices and add enough flour to form a thick batter. Mix well.

2 Add the rest of the flour a little at a time until the dough forms a ball that leaves the sides of the bowl. Knead until smooth, then cover the bowl and place in the refrigerator for about 1 hour.

3 Roll out the dough about ¼ inch (5mm) thick. Cut round a cardboard gingerbread man shape (see below) or use a bought cutter.

4 Transfer the gingerbread figures on to a greased baking sheet and decorate them with currants and almond flakes for eyes, buttons and any other fancy touches. Press the fruit and nuts in firmly so that they stay in place.

5 Bake in a preheated moderate oven 180°C (350°F/Gas Mark 4), for 15–20 minutes. Cool them on a wire rack.

4 fl oz (100ml) soya oil
4 fl oz (100ml) water
3 fl oz (75ml) clear honey
2 fl oz (50ml) molasses or
    black treacle
a pinch sea salt
1 level teaspoon bicarbonate
    of soda
1 tablespoon ground ginger
½ teaspoon ground
    cinnamon
⅛ teaspoon ground cloves
12-14 oz (350-400g) 100
    percent plain, fine-milled
    wholemeal pastry flour
currants and almond flakes,
    to decorate

Note
If you intend to hang your gingerbread figures from the Christmas tree in the traditional way, take a skewer and make a hole in the top of each figure before baking. When cold, thread a narrow ribbon through each hole and hang on the tree.

Gift wrap
Arrange carefully in a box lined with tissue paper and add a roll of ribbon. Wrap the box with Christmas paper. Don't forget to include an instruction card, explaining that the ribbon should be threaded through the hole in the top of each biscuit and then tied carefully to the branches of the tree.

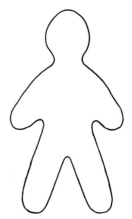

Pattern for a Gingerbread Man.

Gift labels and tree decorations

Use the Gingerbread Men dough (see page 61).

These edible labels could be used to accompany a box of biscuits, or to tie on to Christmas or birthday presents. There are lots of different shapes you can use for tree decorations (see opposite). They are a good way of using up left-over dough.

1 Roll the dough until it is about ¼ inch (5mm) thick, and after cutting out the shapes make a hole for ribbon before baking as for the Gingerbread Men.
2 When cool, carefully thread a piece of ribbon through the hole and tie a small bow. Ice the gift labels with the recipient's name.

For the icing:
2 egg whites
¼ teaspoon cream of tartar
3 oz (75g) clear honey
1 teaspoon vanilla essence
9¾ oz (275g) skimmed milk powder
natural food colouring

1 Whisk the egg whites and cream of tartar together in a bowl until foamy. Whisk in the honey and vanilla essence.
2 Gradually beat in the skimmed milk powder. If the icing is not thick enough, add a little more skimmed milk powder. To tint the icing, add a few drops of natural food colouring.
3 Place the mixture into a piping bag fitted with a writing nozzle, then write the recipient's name or message on the cookie shapes.

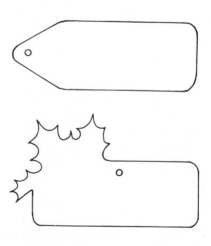

Gift Label Shapes

Tree Decoration Shapes

5.
Cakes and Teabreads

Cakes and teabreads are always presentable and readily accepted, especially among friends and relatives who may not have the time to bake themselves but still enjoy the tastes of good home baking. This chapter offers a wide selection of cakes — there is a cake to suit every occasion. If someone actually goes to the trouble of baking a cake specially for family or friends, the recipient cannot fail to feel spoiled and loved.

Fruit cakes which store well in airtight tins and actually improve with age, are good candidates. Most cakes and teabreads freeze successfully, so goods for giving may be baked well in advance. They can be packed, while frozen, in airtight containers or placed in plastic food bags before being gift-wrapped.

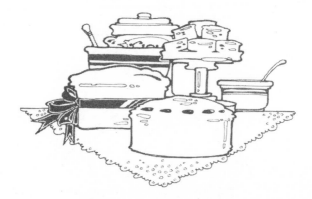

Opposite Dip into some savoury cocktail nibbles (pages 43-9).

Overleaf For Valentine's Day, make the one you love some heart-shaped cookies (see page 59).

Dark ginger cake

Makes a 1 lb 12oz (800g) loaf cake

1 Base line and grease a 7¼ inch × 4½ inch × 3½ inch (18cm × 11.5cm × 8.5cm) loaf tin.

2 Mix together the flour, ginger, mustard powder, cinnamon and baking powder, then set aside.

3 In another bowl, beat together the oil, molasses, malt extract, honey, eggs and milk.

4 Fold the dry ingredients into the beaten mixture.

5 Pour into the prepared tin and bake on the bottom shelf of a preheated cool oven 150°C (300°F/Gas Mark 2), for 1¼–1½ hours, or until a skewer inserted into the cake comes out clean. Turn out on to a wire rack and leave until completely cold before removing the lining paper. Store in an airtight tin until ready for packing.

8 oz (225g) fine milled wholemeal flour
1 level tablespoon ground ginger
1 teaspoon mustard powder
1 level teaspoon ground cinnamon
1 teaspoon salt-free baking powder
7 fl oz (200ml) soya oil
3 fl oz (75ml) molasses
3 fl oz (75ml) malt extract
2 fl oz (50ml) clear honey
2 free-range eggs, beaten
4 fl oz (100ml) skimmed milk

Gift wrap
Wrap in greaseproof paper, then wrap in a checked tea-towel or a square of gingham trimmed round the edges with pinking shears.

Overleaf Give a Simnel Cake (page 76) for an Easter present, or make a Honey Apricot Loaf (page 68).

Opposite Tempt your recipient with these mouth-watering sweets (pages 77-86).

Banana, date and pecan loaf

4 oz (100g) unsalted butter or soft vegetable margarine

3 oz (75g) light muscovado sugar

2 large free-range eggs, well beaten

3 large ripe bananas, peeled

8 oz (225g) wholemeal flour

½ teaspoon ground cinnamon

2 level teaspoons baking powder

3 oz (75g) chopped dates

2 oz (50g) pecans

1 Cream the butter or margarine and sugar until light and fluffy. Beat in the eggs a little at a time.

2 In a separate bowl, mash the bananas to a pulp with a fork, then beat them into the creamed mixture.

3 Sift in the flour and baking powder, adding the bran left in the sieve. Fold into the creamed mixture. Stir in the dates and pecans and mix well.

4 Spoon the mixture into an oiled and base-lined 2lb (900g) loaf tin. Bake in a preheated moderate oven 180°C (350°F/Gas Mark 4), for 1-1¼ hours until firm to the touch.

5 Leave the loaf to cool in the tin for 5 minutes, then turn it out onto a wire cooling rack. This loaf is best kept for 24 hours before cutting.

Gift wrap

Wrap the loaf in foil and pack in a rigid container. Alternatively, stand the loaf on a wooden board, add a knife and wrap with Cellophane for a more costly present. If you are superstitious, ask the recipient to give you a penny for the knife, to prevent a break in the friendship!

Carob yule log

1 Line and lightly oil a 7×11 inch (18×28cm) Swiss roll tin.

2 Whisk the eggs and sugar in a mixing bowl over a pan of hot water until thick enough to leave the trail of the whisk for 3 seconds. Whisk in the water. (Hot water is unnecessary if using an electric beater.) Sift the flour and carob powder, then sieve again on to the egg mixture. Tip in the remaining bran, and fold all together carefully using a metal spoon. Pour into the prepared tin.

3 Bake in the centre of a preheated moderately hot oven, 220°C (425°F/Gas Mark 7), for 8–10 minutes, until the sponge is beginning to shrink away from the sides of the tin and springs back when touched.

4 Turn out on to a sheet of greaseproof paper set on a damp teatowel, peel off the lining paper and trim the edges. Mark a line ½ inch (1cm) in from the edge, along the short edge nearest you, then spread lightly with jam. Roll up quickly, using the greaseproof paper to help you. Leave the Swiss roll wrapped in the paper to cool.

5 Place the Swiss roll on a rectangular silver cake board ready to be 'iced'.

6 To make the frosting, melt the carob pieces in a bowl suspended over a pan of hot water. In a separate bowl, beat the curd cheese to soften it. Pour the melted carob into the cheese and, working quickly, cream them together.

7 With a palette knife, cover the top and sides of the log before the frosting stiffens too much, and mark lines with a fork to resemble the bark of a tree. Decorate as desired with a robin, holly, etc.

3 free-range eggs
3 oz (75g) muscovado sugar
1 tablespoon boiling water
2½ oz (65g) fine-milled wholemeal flour
1 oz (25g) carob powder
3 tablespoons no-added-sugar black cherry jam, for filling

Frosting
3 oz (75g) no-added-sugar plain carob bar, broken into pieces
8 oz (225g) low-fat curd cheese

Honey apricot loaf

Makes a 2 lb (900g) loaf

4-6 oz (100-175g) dried apricots, chopped
5 fl oz (150ml) unsweetened apple juice
5 fl oz (150ml) soya oil
6 fl oz (175ml) clear honey
2 free-range eggs
pinch sea salt
2 teaspoons ground cinnamon
1½ teaspoons baking powder
10 oz (275g) fine wholemeal flour

1 Soak the apricots in the apple juice overnight. Drain and keep the juice.
2 Put the oil, apple juice, honey and eggs into a large bowl and beat them all together until smooth.
3 Mix the salt, cinnamon and baking powder with the flour before adding to the liquid ingredients. Add the apricots and mix well.
4 Pour the mixture into a lightly-oiled 2 lb (900g) base-lined loaf tin. Bake in a preheated moderate oven, 170°C (325°F/Gas Mark 3), for 45–50 minutes or until a skewer inserted into the centre of the cake comes out clean. Turn out on to a wire rack and peel away the lining paper when cold. Store in an airtight tin until ready for packing.

Gift wrap
If you feel like making someone a present of a baking tin as well as the cake, pop the cake back into the tin in which it was baked. Cover with non-PVC cling-film and wrap in fancy paper. Tie like a parcel, using ribbon and finish off with a large bow.

Passion cake

Makes one 8 inch (20cm) cake

1 In a large bowl, mix together the flour, sugar, sultanas or raisins, walnuts, desiccated coconut, cinnamon, nutmeg and mixed spice.

2 Finely grate the carrots into the mixture.

3 Beat together the eggs, honey, bananas and oil. Stir into the dry ingredients, beating well as the mixture loosens.

4 Turn into a lined and greased 8-inch (20cm) round cake tin and bake in a preheated moderate oven, 170°C (325°F/Gas Mark 3), for 1¼–1½ hours or until a skewer inserted into the centre of the cake comes out clean.

5 Remove the cake from the oven and leave to cool in the tin for about 5 minutes. Turn out on to a wire rack and peel away the lining paper. Leave the cake until completely cold before storing in an airtight tin (up to 3 days) in readiness for packing.

Gift wrap
Follow directions for Honey Apricot Loaf (see opposite). Alternatively, place the cake in a large square of coloured Cellophane paper. Draw edges together over the top of the cake and tie with ribbon, finishing off with a large bow.

10 oz (275g) fine self-raising wholemeal flour
3 oz (75g) muscovado sugar
3 oz (75g) sultanas or raisins
3 oz (75g) walnuts, chopped
2 oz (50g) desiccated coconut
1 teaspoon ground cinnamon
¼ teaspoon ground nutmeg
¼ teaspoon ground mixed spice
8 oz (225g) carrots
2 large free-range eggs
3 tablespoons clear honey
2 large ripe bananas, mashed
6 fl oz (175ml) soya or sunflower oil

Carob and almond cake

Makes a 7 inch (18cm) cake

6 oz (175g) no-added-sugar plain carob bar, broken into pieces
4 oz (100g) unsalted butter, softened
3 oz (75g) dark muscovado sugar
4 free-range eggs, separated
1½ oz (40g) ground almonds
3 tablespoons dark rum
a few drops almond essence
2½ oz (65g) 85 per cent self-raising wholemeal flour, sieved
4 tablespoons no-added-sugar apricot jam, for filling

Icing
2 tablespoons water
3 oz (75g) no-added-sugar plain carob bar, broken into pieces
1 oz (25g) unsalted butter
flaked almonds, to decorate

1 Put the broken carob bar into a bowl, then place the bowl over a saucepan of barely simmering water and leave it to melt slowly, being careful not to let it overheat.
2 Cream the butter and sugar until light and fluffy. Gradually beat in the egg yolks, a little at a time, beating well after each addition. Then add the melted carob, the ground almonds, rum and the almond essence. Mix well.
3 Whisk the egg whites until stiff and holding firm peaks. Fold in 2 tablespoons of the egg whites to lighten the mixture, then fold in the flour. Finally fold in the remaining egg white mixture.
4 Divide the mixture between two lightly-oiled and lined 7-inch (18cm) sandwich tins. Bake in a preheated moderate oven, 180°C (350°F/Gas Mark 4), for about 25 minutes or until just firm to the touch. Cool on a wire rack. When cold, sandwich together with the jam.
5 Place the water and broken carob bar in a bowl over a saucepan of simmering water, and stir until the carob is melted. Take off the heat and beat in the butter. Allow to cool slightly, then spread over the whole of the cake using a palette knife to cover the top and sides completely. Sprinkle flaked almonds on top and leave to set.

Gift wrap
Place the cake on a doily-covered cake board and transfer to a cardboard box. Pad round with crumpled tissue paper, then wrap with Cellophane paper. Decorate with a spray of artificial or fresh flowers.

Almond slices

Makes 10

1 Rub the butter or margarine into the flour until the mixture resembles fine breadcrumbs. Add the egg yolk and just enough cold water to mix to a soft, but not sticky dough.

2 Roll the dough out to line an 8-inch (20cm) shallow square cake tin and flute the edges. Spread the base with jam.

3 For the topping: cream the margarine with the sugar until light and fluffy. Beat in the eggs a little at a time (if necessary add some of the soya flour to prevent curdling). Add the almond essence. Mix in the soya flour and baking powder. Spread the mixture carefully over the jam.

4 Sprinkle flaked almonds on top and bake in a preheated moderate oven, 170°C (325°F/Gas Mark 3), for 50–60 minutes, until well risen and golden brown. Leave to cool in the tin and then mark into slices.

Gift wrap
Make in a new tin and give with the cake, or cut into slices and pack attractively in a box.

Pastry
3 oz (75g) unsalted butter or soft vegetable margarine
6 oz (175g) fine-milled wholemeal pastry flour
1 free-range egg yolk
cold water, to mix
4 tablespoons no-added-sugar apricot jam, for filling

Topping
3 oz (75g) soft vegetable margarine
3 oz (75g) light muscovado sugar
2 free-range eggs, beaten
3 oz (75g) soya flour, sifted
½ teaspoon almond essence
½ teaspoon baking powder, sifted
1 oz (25g) flaked almonds

Boston brownies

Makes 16 pieces

6 oz (175g) no-added-sugar
  plain carob bars
4 oz (100g) unsalted butter or
  margarine
3 free-range eggs
3 oz (75g) dark muscovado
2 tablespoons clear honey
1 teaspoon vanilla essence
4 oz (100g) 100 percent self-
  raising wholemeal flour
2 oz (50g) seedless raisins
2 oz (50g) chopped walnuts
5 tablespoons double cream

1 Put 3 oz (75g) chopped carob bar and the butter or margarine in a heatproof bowl and place over a pan of simmering water. Stir until melted and cool slightly.
2 Meanwhile, beat the eggs, sugar, honey and vanilla essence until light and frothy, then add the cooled carob and butter mixture. Stir in the flour, then add the raisins and chopped walnuts and mix well.
3 Pour the mixture into a shallow 8 × 10 inch (20 × 25cm) cake tin which has been lined with greased greaseproof paper.
4 Bake in the centre of a preheated moderate oven, 180°C (350°F/Gas Mark 4), for 25–30 minutes, until firm to the touch. Cool in the tin.
5 Put the cream into a small pan and bring to the boil. Remove from the heat, add the remaining chopped carob bar and stir until completely melted and smooth. Pour over the cake in the tin and smooth the top with a spatula or palette knife. When set cut into squares or fingers.

Gift wrap
Pack in a shallow rectangular box lined with foil. Cover with a lid or wrap with more foil, then decorate with blue and red stars and stripes, cut from coloured gummed paper, to represent the American flag.

Dundee cake

Makes a 7 inch (18cm) cake

1 Place the chopped dates in a small saucepan with the water and cook gently for 5-10 minutes to make a purée. Leave to cool.

2 Blend the butter or margarine, eggs and cooked dates together until smooth and creamy. Sieve in the flour, baking powder and spice, adding the bran remaining in the sieve. Mix well.

3 Add the currants, sultanas, mixed peel, cherries, ground almonds and lemon rind. Stir the ingredients until they are thoroughly mixed.

4 Spoon the mixture into an oiled and lined 7 inch (18cm) round cake tin, making a shallow dip in the centre, so that the cake will rise evenly. Arrange the whole almonds in circles all over the top.

5 Bake in the centre of a preheated moderate oven, 160°C (325°F/Gas Mark 3), for 2-2½ hours, or until a skewer inserted in the centre comes out clean. Allow the cake to cool slightly before turning it out of the tin on a wire rack to cool completely.

6 Remove the lining paper, then wrap in fresh greaseproof paper. Store the cake in an airtight tin until ready for packing.

6 oz (175g) cooking dates
¼ pint (150ml) water
4 oz (100g) unsalted butter or soft vegetable margarine
3 free-range eggs
8 oz (225g) plain wholemeal flour
2 teaspoons baking powder
1 teaspoon ground mixed spice
6 oz (175g) currants
6 oz (175g) sultanas
2 oz (50g) mixed candied peel, finely chopped
2 oz (50g) undyed glacé cherries, halved
1 oz (25g) ground almonds
grated rind of ½ lemon
1½ oz (40g) split blanched almonds, to decorate

Gift wrap
Pack in a box, then tie with tartan ribbon and attach a miniature bottle of whisky and a sprig of heather.

Guinness cake

8 oz (225g) dried dates, pitted and chopped
¼ pint (150ml) plus 4 tablespoons Guinness
6 oz (175g) unsalted butter, softened
4 free-range eggs, beaten
12 oz (350g) 100 percent wholemeal flour
2 teaspoons ground mixed spice
2 teaspoons baking powder
6 oz (175g) seedless raisins
6 oz (175g) currants
3 oz (75g) walnuts, not too finely chopped

1 Place the chopped dates in a pan with ¼ pint (150ml) of Guinness and cook gently for 5–10 minutes until soft. Leave for 10 minutes.

2 Blend the butter, eggs and cooked dates together until smooth and creamy.

3 Sift together the flour, spice and baking powder, adding the bran left in the sieve, and gradually fold in the blended ingredients. Add the raisins, currants and the chopped walnuts. It may be necessary to add a little more Guinness if the mixture is very stiff. Mix well.

4 Spoon into an oiled and lined 8-inch (20cm) round cake tin, making a small hollow in the centre of the mixture, to ensure even rising.

5 Bake in the centre of a preheated cool oven, 150°C (300°F/Gas Mark 2), for 2–2¼ hours, or until the top of the cake is brown and firm to the touch. Leave the cake to cool in the tin for 15 minutes before turning out onto a wire rack.

6 When the cake is cold, turn it upside down and prick the base with a thin skewer. Gradually spoon over the remaining Guinness and when it has all been absorbed wrap the cake in greaseproof paper and foil and store in an airtight tin for 2–3 days to mature before giving away.

Gift wrap
Leave the cake in foil, then wrap in a novelty tea-towel. Tie up like a parcel with ribbon and finish off with a bow.

Christmas cake

1 Place the dried fruit in a bowl with the flaked almonds, lemon rind and sherry or orange juice, cover with a damp cloth and leave to stand for 8 hours or overnight.

2 Grease an 8 inch (20cm) round cake tin or a 7 inch (18cm) square tin and line the base and sides with a double layer of greased greaseproof paper. Tie a thick band of brown paper around the outside of the tin and stand it on a pad of brown paper on a baking sheet to protect the cake during cooking.

3 Cream the butter, sugar and molasses together until light and fluffy. Gradually beat in the eggs, a little at a time, adding the ground almonds alternately and mixing well after each addition.

4 Sieve the flour and spices into the bowl, adding any bran remaining in the sieve. Add the fruit, then the milk and mix to a dropping consistency.

5 Spoon into the prepared tin and smooth the top. Cover the top loosely with several layers of greaseproof paper and a layer of brown paper.

6 Bake in a preheated cool oven, 140°C (275°F/Gas Mark 1). Check the cake after 2½ hours, and then at half hourly intervals. Test by inserting a skewer into the centre of the cake; if it emerges clean then the cake is ready.

7 Remove from the oven and leave to cool in the tin until completely cold. Remove from tin, and take out of the lining paper. Wrap in kitchen foil and store in an airtight container until needed.

8 Arrange the nut halves on the top of the cake. Make a glaze by combining the apricot jam with the honey and boiling water in a small bowl. This makes a smooth, shiny paste. Brush this over the top of the cake.

Gift wrap
Tie a decorative cake band around the cake and top with a sprig of holly, then wrap in Cellophane paper.

8 oz (225g) currants
6 oz (175g) raisins
4 oz (100g) sultanas
3 oz (75g) dried apricots, finely chopped
3 oz (75g) flaked almonds
grated rind 1 lemon
3 tablespoons dry sherry or orange juice
6 oz (175g) soft vegetable margarine or unsalted butter
4 oz (100g) molasses sugar
1 tablespoon molasses
4 large free-range eggs
2 oz (50g) ground almonds
7 oz (200g) wholemeal flour
1 level teaspoon ground mixed spice
½ teaspoon ground cinnamon
¼ teaspoon ground nutmeg
1 tablespoon milk

To decorate
2 tablespoons no-added-sugar apricot jam
2 tablespoons clear honey
2 tablespoons boiling water
a selection of shelled nuts to arrange round the cake — pecans, walnuts, Brazils and almonds — all halved

Simnel cake

This rich fruit cake was originally given by girls in Shrewsbury as a gift to their mothers on Mothering Sunday. However it is now a traditional favourite at Easter. The eleven balls represent the apostles at The Last Supper. (The missing twelfth ball is Judas Iscariot, who has slipped away from the meal to betray his Master.) This cake has a layer of marzipan in the middle.

Makes one 7½ inch (19cm) cake

6 oz (175g) unsalted butter or soft vegetable margarine
5 oz (150g) light muscovado sugar
3 large free-range eggs
8 oz (225g) wholemeal flour
1 teaspoon baking powder
2 oz (50g) ground almonds
2 teaspoons ground mixed spice
6 oz (175g) currants
6 oz (175g) sultanas
2 oz (50g) undyed glacé cherries, quartered
2 oz (50g) candied orange and lemon peel, chopped into small pieces
grated rind of 1 orange
3 tablespoons brandy or milk
1¼ lb (550g) raw sugar marzipan, shop bought or homemade

To finish:
1 tablespoon raw sugar apricot jam
beaten egg white, to glaze

1 Cream together the butter or margarine and sugar until light and fluffy. Beat in the eggs, a little at a time, adding a little of the weighed flour if necessary to prevent curdling.
2 Sift in the remaining flour, baking powder, the ground almonds and spice and sprinkle in the bran remaining in the sieve. Add the currants, sultanas, cherries, candied peel and grated orange rind and gradually fold these ingredients in, using a metal spoon. Add the milk or brandy and mix to a soft dropping consistency.
3 Roll out one-third of the marzipan to a 7½ inch (19cm) round. Place half the cake mixture into a 7½ inch (19cm) greased and lined round cake tin and cover with the round of marzipan. Top with the remaining cake mixture and level the surface. Bake in a preheated moderate oven, 160°C (325°F/Gas Mark 3) for 1 hour, then lower the temperature to 150°C (300°F/Gas Mark 2) and bake for a further 2½ hours or until a skewer inserted into the centre comes out clean. Cool in the tin, then turn out and remove paper.
4 Roll out half of the remaining marzipan to a 7½ inch (19cm) round. Brush with apricot jam and press on to the top of the cake. Flute the edges. Use the remaining paste to make 11 small balls and place them at regular intervals around the edge of the cake with a dab of beaten egg white. Brush over the whole surface with more egg white. Toast the marzipan layer under a hot grill for a few minutes to colour it lightly, taking care not to allow it to burn. This cake keeps beautifully in an airtight tin so it can be made well in advance.

6.
Sweets

Home-made sweets are ideal for giving as gifts with that truly personal touch. They are a joy to make and a real delight to receive. With home-made sweets, you will never be at a loss for something to give, whatever the recipient's age or taste.

Making sweets is also something that children can enjoy and they can help, or do it themselves under supervision, making the results especially acceptable for grandparents.

Clear glass jars with screw-top or ground glass closures are ideal for showing off sweets that do not crush easily. If giving the sweets as a present tie a ribbon and bow around the neck of the jar and decorate the body of the jar with cut-out shapes of coloured paper. Store all sweets in a cool, dry place until ready for packing.

Apricot and coconut balls

Makes 34

8 oz (225g) dried apricots
3 oz (85g) desiccated
coconut
1 teaspoon grated orange
rind
1 teaspoon grated lemon rind
2 dessertspoons orange juice
1 oz (25g) desiccated
coconut, for rolling

1 In a small saucepan, cook apricots covered with water until soft. Drain, dry on paper towels and chop.
2 Mix the apricots with the coconut, then either put through a food mill, using a medium-sized disc, or place in a food processor. Add the orange and lemon rind and the orange juice. Knead into a soft, slightly moist paste.
3 Form the mixture into marble-sized balls. Roll in the coconut. Refrigerate until firm. Store covered with foil between layers in the refrigerator for up to 10 days.

Gift wrap
Pack in a single layer, in a doily-lined box. Either cover with a lid if it fits, or wrap in Cellophane. Add a ribbon bow.

Fruit and nut truffles

Makes 20

2 oz (50g) stoned dates
2 oz (50g) dried figs
3 oz (75g) seedless raisins
3 oz (75g) dried apricots
2 oz (50g) chopped walnuts
1 tablespoon lemon juice
1 tablespoon clear honey
(optional)
1 oz (25g) desiccated
coconut, for tossing

1 Mince or very finely chop the dates, figs, raisins and apricots. Stir in the chopped nuts, lemon juice and honey (if using). Press the mixture together in a bowl. The mixture should bind together when pressed between fingers. If too firm, moisten with more lemon juice.
2 Using the palms of the hands, roll the mixture into balls about 1 inch (2.5cm) in diameter. Roll each ball in the desiccated coconut to coat completely.
3 Chill for 2 hours on a plate. Refrigerate in a covered container in a single layer or with foil between layers for up to 3 weeks.

Gift wrap
As Apricot and Coconut Balls (see above).

Fruit and nut clusters

Makes about 24 clusters

These sweets are very simple to make. A little of your favourite liqueur can be added to the melted carob to make them even more special.

1 Melt the carob in a bowl suspended over hot water, (take care the bowl does not actually touch the water). Remove from the heat and stir in the fruit, nuts and peel and mix thoroughly.
2 Place teaspoonfuls of the mixture on to non-stick baking parchment or greaseproof paper, or into paper sweet-cases and leave to set.

6 oz (175g) plain no-added-sugar carob bar, broken into pieces
3 oz (75g) large seedless raisins
3 oz (75g) toasted hazelnuts, coarsely chopped
1 oz (25g) candied lemon or orange peel, chopped
petit-four cases

Variation
Date and Walnut Clusters. Make this delicious version at Christmas when dates are plentiful. Use 3 oz (75g) chopped dates instead of the raisins and 3 oz (75g) chopped walnuts instead of hazelnuts. Follow the recipe above.

Gift wrap
If made in paper sweet-cases, layer into a fancy box with greaseproof paper between layers. Cover with a lid or wrap with Cellophane paper. Alternatively, pack fine strips of coloured Cellophane paper in the bottom of a mug to form a 'nest' and over-wrap it, together with the fruit and nut clusters that are piled up, with Cellophane paper to hold them in place. Tie with ribbon.

Hazelnut clusters

6 oz (175g) shelled hazelnuts
6 oz (175g) plain no-added-sugar carob bars, broken into pieces

1 Spread the hazelnuts in a single layer on a baking sheet. Place in a preheated moderate oven, 180°C (350°F/Gas Mark 4). Roast the nuts for about 10 minutes. Shake and stir frequently. Turn into a clean tea-towel and rub off the loose skins. Leave the nuts to cool.

2 Melt the carob in the top of a double boiler or in a bowl suspended over a pan of hot water. When completely melted, remove from the heat and stir in the hazelnuts, coating thoroughly.

3 Using a teaspoon, retrieve four nuts at a time with a good portion of carob. Place the mixture in small spoonfuls in paper sweet-cases or in little heaps on waxed or non-stick parchment paper until set.

Variation
Use whole shelled peanuts, raisins or almond nibs as an alternative.

Gift wrap
Transfer to paper cases and pack, in a single layer, in a decorative box. Top with a lid if it fits, or wrap in coloured Cellophane. Add a trimming of ribbon. Alternatively, layer carefully into a chunky glass jar with stopper. Tie with a ribbon at the neck and finish off with a bow.

Opposite Why not try preserving your recipient's favourite fruits in alcohol? (See pages 87-95.)

Carob-coated stuffed dates

Makes 20

1 With a small sharp knife slit along the length of each date and carefully lift out the stone.
2 Make the almond paste by mixing together the almonds and sugar. Add the sherry or lemon juice and enough egg white to mix to a smooth pliable paste, then form it into small pieces that will fit into the cavities in the dates left by the stones.
3 Stuff each date with a little paste. Press the date together so that the almond paste is firmly enclosed.
4 Melt the carob in a bowl over a pan of simmering water and, with the aid of two forks, dip the dates in the carob. Coat evenly and brush off any surplus on the edge of the bowl. Place on greaseproof paper to set. Store, covered in the refrigerator for up to 2 weeks.

20 well-shaped dried dates
8 oz (225g) plain no-added-
  sugar carob bar

For the almond paste
4 oz (100g) ground almonds
2 oz (50g) light muscovado
  sugar
1 teaspoon sherry or lemon
  juice
egg white, to mix

Stuffed walnuts

1 Form the almond paste into thick discs, then sandwich between two walnut halves.
2 Place in small paper sweet-cases.

1 quantity of almond paste
  (see recipe above) or use
  shop bought raw sugar
  marzipan
walnut halves

Opposite A selection of delicious gifts for that special occasion.
(For more ideas see pages 96-108.)

Carob cherry bells

Makes about 24

These carob cherry bells are a little time consuming to make, but they really are worth the trouble. Make them for a very special gift or serve them with coffee after dinner.

24 sour cherries, stoned
2 tablespoons kirsch, brandy or cognac
1 packet 6 small plastic Christmas bells (see note below)
8 oz (225g) plain no-added-sugar carob bar, broken in pieces

1 Combine the cherries and kirsch, brandy or cognac in a small bowl. Cover and refrigerate for 3 days. Stir occasionally. Drain the cherries and reserve the liqueur.
2 Wash and dry the bells thoroughly.
3 Place the carob in the top of a double boiler or in a heatproof bowl over a saucepan of hot but not boiling water. Heat gently until melted, stirring occasionally.
4 Put a small amount of carob inside the bell and rotate the bell so that the melted carob runs around the inside, completely coating the inside of the bell. Refrigerate until set.
5 When set, place a cherry inside the bell and add a few drops of the reserved liqueur, then spread a little more melted carob to seal the bell completely. Refrigerate until set.
6 To unmould, insert a small, fine skewer into the top part of the bell. This will break the seal of the carob inside the bell, allowing it to be removed without difficulty.
7 Using a skewer, drop a small amount of melted carob on top of each bell, then place a small ribbon bow in position. These bells will remain solid at room temperature.

Note
The small plastic Christmas bells used can be obtained from chain stores in packets of 6.

Rum and raisin cups

Makes 24

1 Put the raisins and rum in a bowl, cover tightly with cling-film and soak overnight.

2 Melt two-thirds of the carob in a bowl over a pan of hot water. Place two small petit-four paper cases together (one inside the other) and put a small amount of melted carob in the bottom. Swirl the melted carob inside the case, making sure that the sides and bottom are fully coated. Turn them upside-down to drain on a wire rack so they set without the carob creeping back down the sides into the bases. Leave for at least 30 minutes.

3 Divide the soaked raisins between the carob-lined cases. Spoon a few drops of the rum into each case. Melt the remaining carob over hot water. Spoon on top of the raisins, making sure that the cups are completely sealed. Before the carob dries, decorate each one with a few flaked almonds. Leave to set.

4 oz (100g) large seedless raisins
4 tablespoons dark rum
12 oz (350g) plain no-added-sugar carob bar
1 oz (25g) flaked almonds, to decorate

Gift wrap
Remove the paper cases and arrange the rum and raisin cups in a single layer, in a doily-lined decorative box, or on a porcelain plate to give as part of the present. Wrap in Cellophane paper, then add a ribbon trimming.

Rum truffles

Makes about 20 balls

6 oz (175g) plain no-added-
sugar carob bar
1 large free-range egg yolk
1 oz (25g) unsalted butter
2 teaspoons rum
1 teaspoon top of the milk or
single cream
carob powder, for dusting

1 Break up the carob into small pieces and place in the top of a double boiler, or a bowl over a pan of hot water (do not let it actually touch the water) and heat until melted.

2 Remove from the heat and beat in the remaining ingredients, except for the carob powder, then chill in the refrigerator until the mixture is firm enough to handle.

3 Sieve some carob powder on to a clean work-surface. Take about a rounded teaspoonful of the mixture, shape it into a ball in the palm of the hands, then lightly roll in the carob powder.

Note
For a sweeter truffle, coat the balls in a mixture of carob powder and finely ground raw cane sugar.

Variation
(See opposite.)

An elegant cluster of grapes

1 Make some of the truffles slightly smaller than the others so that there are a variety of sizes. Arrange the truffles in a cluster on a small serving platter, with the smallest ones at the bottom, the larger truffles stacked at the top.

2 Melt 4 oz (100g) plain no-added-sugar carob bar over hot water. Line a baking sheet with non-stick parchment paper. Select a very large ivy or grape leaf, and brush the melted carob over the back of the leaf. Place the leaf on the baking sheet to set.

3 Put the remaining melted carob into a small paper piping bag, and make a rough grape stem 3 inches (7.5cm) long and ¾ inch (2 cm) wide, with a slight curve to it. Pipe out a long, spiralling tendril. Place the baking sheet in the refrigerator to harden for 5 minutes.

4 Peel off the leaf from the carob and remove the stem and tendrils. Arrange them at the top of the cluster.

Rum truffles (see opposite)
4 oz (100g) plain no-added sugar carob bar
ivy or grape leaf

Collettes

4 oz (100g) plain no-added-
sugar carob bar
small foil petit-four cases
1 oz (25g) chopped pistachio
nuts

Filling
3½ oz (90g) plain no-added-
sugar carob bar
1 oz (25g) unsalted butter
2 teaspoons Armagnac or
brandy
2 fl oz (60ml) double cream

1 Break up the first lot of carob into small pieces and place in the top of a double boiler, or a bowl suspended over a pan of simmering water, and heat until melted.
2 Spread the inside of the small foil cases with the carob using a brush or back of a teaspoon. Turn cases upside-down on a plate. Refrigerate until set, then peel away the foil cases if desired.
3 Melt the remaining carob with the butter and leave until cool but not set, then stir in the Armagnac or brandy.
4 Whisk the cream until stiff and fold in the carob mixture. Leave until thick enough for piping.
5 Spoon the filling into a piping bag fitted with a fluted nozzle or star tube and pipe into the carob cases. Sprinkle with chopped pistachio nuts. Store, covered, in the refrigerator for up to 1 week.

Gift wrap
Transfer to paper sweet-cases and arrange, in single layer, in a fancy box lined with tissue paper or doilies. Cover with a lid or wrap in coloured Cellophane paper. Add a ribbon bow.

7.
Fruits in Alcohol

Colourful jars of clementines in Armagnac, pineapple rings in kirsch, figs in port, prunes steeped in sherry, all are bottled fruit with a difference. With fruits in alcohol, the spirit used in the recipe is the preservative. Even though this makes them expensive, the results are delicious and are much less costly to make at home than they are to buy in high-quality food shops.

Use the best fruit possible — anything else doesn't justify the expense — and leave the fruits to steep in a cool, dark place. Proper preserving jars are essential to eliminate all possibility of evaporation. These have wide necks that make it easier to pack in the prepared fruit.

Brandy is the traditional preservative, but whisky, rum or sherry may be used where it complements the fruit. These luxurious preserved fruits make delightful gifts for friends or relatives, especially at Christmas.

Sterilizing the jars
Wash the jars in hot soapy water and thoroughly rinse them, then stand on a trivet or rack in a large pan of water and bring to the boil. Remove the jars from the pan, stand upside-down to drain, then put into a low oven, 130°C (250°F/Gas Mark ½), to dry.

Dried apricots in Marsala

Fills two 16 fl oz (500ml) preserving jars

1 lb (450g) whole dried
  apricots
4 oz (100g) light muscovado
  sugar
rind of 1 lemon, cut into
  strips
about ¼ pint (150ml) dry
  Marsala wine

1 Sterilize two 16 fl oz (500ml) preserving jars (see page 87) and put them in a low oven to keep warm until needed.

2 Put the apricots, sugar and lemon peel in a pan with 1¾ pints (1 litre) of water. Bring slowly to the boil, stirring occasionally to dissolve the sugar. Boil for 10 minutes to reduce the volume of syrup slightly.

3 Reduce the heat and simmer the fruit until tender (about 30 minutes). Drain them and reserve the liquid. Allow the fruit to cool.

4 Pack the apricots into the warm jars allowing room for them to expand in the delicious syrup. Divide the Marsala between the jars, then fill up with the reserved syrup to within ½ inch (1cm) of the top. If the syrup runs short fill the jars with more Marsala. Seal the jars and tip them gently to mix the liquids together.

5 Store in a cool, dark place and allow to mature for at least 3 weeks before opening. They will keep up to 3 months.

Gift label
Eat warmed in their own syrup, with cream or a thick creamy yogurt.

Variation
Use dried peach halves in place of the apricots.

Figs in port

Fills a 16 fl oz (500ml) preserving jar

1 Place the figs in a single layer in a large saucepan or frying pan with the sugar and cinnamon stick. Just cover with water and poach very gently over low heat for about 5 minutes. Remove from the heat and drain, reserving the syrup but removing the cinnamon stick.

2 Pack the figs into a sterilized (see page 87) 16 fl oz (500ml) preserving jar. Reduce the syrup to half by simmering uncovered.

3 Pour the port over the figs and enough syrup to cover, and seal. Tip the jar gently to mix the liquids. Store in a cool, dark place and allow to mature for at least 1 month before using.

9 oz (250g) dried whole figs
4 oz (100g) light muscovado sugar
1 cinnamon stick
about ⅓ pint (200ml) port

Clementines in Armagnac

Makes two 1¼ pint (700ml) jars

2 lb (900g) clementines, scrubbed and leaves, stalks and flower-ends removed
1 pint (600ml) water
4 oz (100g) demerara sugar
vanilla pod
Armagnac or brandy

1 Prick the clementines all over with a sterilized darning needle so that the syrup can penetrate the skins.

2 Put the water and sugar in a saucepan, add the vanilla pod and stir over low heat until the sugar has completely dissolved. Boil for 10 minutes.

3 Add the clementines and bring back to the boil, simmer, uncovered (turning the fruit over occasionally) for 25 minutes, or until the skins feel soft. Pierce them with a fine skewer to test.

4 Meanwhile, sterilize two 1¼ pint (700ml) preserving jars (see page 87) and put them in a low oven, 130°C (250°F/Gas Mark ½), to keep warm until they are needed.

5 Using a perforated spoon, lift out the clementines and pack them into warm jars. Pour in sufficient Armagnac or brandy to come three quarters of the way up the fruit. Top up with the syrup from the pan which has been allowed to cool a little. Add half of the vanilla pod to each jar.

6 Seal with a screw- or clip-top. Tip them gently to mix the liquids together. Store in a cool, dark place and allow to mellow for at least 4 weeks before using.

Kumquats in curaçao

1 Sterilize a 1¼ pint (700ml) glass preserving jar (see page 87) and put it into a low oven, 130°C (250°F/Gas Mark ½), to keep warm until needed.
2 Wash and dry the kumquats, then prick them all over with a fork so that the alcohol can penetrate the skins.
3 Place a layer of kumquats in the base of the warmed jar, sprinkle with some of the sugar, then continue layering the fruit and sugar until the jar is almost full.
4 Pour in the curaçao so that it completely covers the fruit and seal the jar tightly. Holding the jar horizontally, shake it from side to side to help the sugar start dissolving. Label and store in a cool, dark place for at least 6 months. During that time, turn the jar upside-down or give it a shake — about once a month will do.

1 lb (450g) kumquats
4 tablespoons demerara
  sugar
¾ pint (425ml) curaçao

Boozy pears

4 large or 6 small, firm pears, such as Williams or Comice
1 tablespoon lemon juice
6 oz (175g) demerara sugar
¾ pint (450ml) dry red or rosé wine
3 whole cloves
1 stick cinnamon

1 Carefully peel whole pears retaining stalks. Brush with the lemon juice to prevent browning. Pack the pears tightly (and neatly) into a warm, sterilized (see page 87) 1¾ pint (1 litre) glass preserving jar with hinged lid.
2 Meanwhile, dissolve the sugar in the wine in a pan, add the cloves and cinnamon. Boil for 1 minute, then pour over the pears to within 1 inch (2.5cm) of the top of the jar. Secure with the metal clip.
3 Place the jar in a tall saucepan with a false bottom (a metal grid or folded coarse cloth is ideal), about 2 inches (5cm) deeper than the height of the jar. Cover with warm water up to the neck. Bring the water to simmering point in 25–30 minutes, and keep simmering for 40 minutes. Remove the jar from water bath with tongs. Cool, label and store.

Pineapple rings in kirsch

Makes two 1¾ pint (1 litre) jars

1 Cut off both ends of each pineapple and remove all the skin, and as many 'eyes' as possible. Slice into rings ¼–½ inch (0.5–1cm) thick; use an apple corer to remove the tough centre of each slice.

2 Sterilize two wide-necked 1¾ pint (1 litre) preserving jars (see page 87) which will just hold the pineapple rings and put them in a low oven, 130°C (250°F/Gas Mark ½), to keep warm.

3 Put the water into a large frying-pan with the sugar and bring it slowly to the boil, stirring occasionally to dissolve the sugar. Boil for 5 minutes.

4 Add the pineapple rings to the syrup and poach gently for 10 minutes. Using a perforated spoon, lift out the rings and pack them into the warm jars.

5 Divide the kirsch equally between the two jars and add enough syrup from the pan to cover the fruit completely. Seal with a screw- or clip-top, and tip gently to mix the liquids. Leave the jars to cool completely.

6 Store in a cool, dark place and allow to mellow for at least 2 weeks before using.

2 large sound, firm
   pineapples
6 oz (175g) demerara sugar
1 pint (600ml) water
½ pint (300ml) kirsch

Brandied cherries

1 lb (450g) Morello cherries
8 oz (225g) muscovado sugar
½ pint (300ml) water
1 cinnamon stick
about ¼ pint (150ml) brandy

1 Trim the cherry stalks to ⅛ inch (3mm). Wash the cherries, then prick all over with a sterilized darning needle or cocktail stick.
2 In a saucepan, combine 4 oz (100g) sugar, water and the cinnamon stick and cook gently until the sugar has dissolved. Bring to the boil. Add the cherries and poach gently for 5 minutes or until tender. Remove from the heat and pack the fruit into sterilized preserving jars using a draining spoon, reserving the syrup.
3 Add the remaining sugar to the reserved syrup and dissolve it slowly. Bring to the boil, and heat to 110°C (230°F) on a sugar thermometer, then allow to cool. Measure the syrup and add an equal quantity of brandy.
4 Pour the syrup over the cherries to cover them completely. Seal tightly and store in a cool, dark place for 3-4 months to allow the fruit to absorb the brandy.

94

Tipsy prunes

Fills two 16 fl oz (500ml) preserving jars

Almost any dried fruits when plumped out with brandy, sherry, port or the like taste delicious. The jars should not be packed too tightly as the fruit swells with the alcohol.

1 Put the sugar, cinnamon sticks, orange peel and water in a pan and bring to the boil, stirring occasionally to dissolve the sugar. Simmer for 15 minutes.

2 Add the prunes and continue to simmer for a further 30 minutes or until they are just tender — you may need to add a little more water.

3 Pack the prunes into sterilized jars, using a slotted spoon. Add the orange peel and pieces of cinnamon to each jar. Pour in sufficient sherry to come half-way up the jars, then fill up with the reserved syrup. Seal the jars and tip them gently to mix the liquids together. Store in a cool, dark place and allow to mellow for 3 weeks. They will keep for up to 3 months.

4 oz (100g) demerara sugar
2 cinnamon sticks
rind of 1 orange, cut into
  strips
1 pint (600ml) water
1 lb (450g) stoned prunes
approximately ½ pint
  (300ml) medium-dry
  sherry

Variation
Dried apricots, peaches, pears or figs also make splendid substitutes for prunes.

8.
Special Presents

Home-made pesents make very special gifts, and giving specially-made gifts of food and drink is one of the nicest ways of showing someone how much you care. A jar of home-made mayonnaise is more likely to be appreciated by a hard-pressed family cook than an expensive box of chocolates. In this chapter you will find recipes to suit all sorts of occasions, including traditional ones like Solid Carob Easter Eggs, Mince Pies and Christmas Puddings, and for those who like dabbling in beer-making there is even one for making a Mild Ale.

Sugar-free mincemeat

Fills four 12 oz (350g) jars

1 Put the apples, dried fruit and apple juice in a saucepan. Cover, bring to the boil and simmer gently for 30 minutes.
2 Blend the miso with a little of the liquid from the pan before adding to the cooked fruit. Stir in the lemon rind, brandy and spices, and leave to cool. Let the mincemeat stand for a day or two before using.
3 Spoon into clean, dry jars and cover. Store in the refrigerator until the time comes for giving away.

Gift wrap
Label jars with decorative or coloured labels, then cover tops with pretty fabric cut round the edges with pinking shears. Tie round with fine cord, ribbon or coloured string.

1¼ lb (550g) eating apples, cored and grated
1 lb (450g) mixed dried vine fruits (raisins, sultanas, currants)
½ pint (300ml) natural unsweetened apple juice
1 tablespoon miso (soya bean paste)
grated rind 1 lemon
2 tablespoons brandy
1 level teaspoon ground cinnamon
½ level teaspoon mixed spice
¼ level teaspoon ground ginger

Yogurt cheese in olive oil

Makes ½ lb (225g)

1 Line a colander or strainer with a square of butter muslin (cheesecloth). Stand it over a bowl. Tip the yogurt into the muslin and tie it up with string, to form a bag. Lift it out of the colander. Tie the strings to a tap over a sink and leave to drain for at least 8 hours or overnight.
2 Mash the yogurt curds with salt and pepper to taste and shape into balls about 1 inch (2.5cm) in diameter. Put these carefully into a glass preserving jar with a hinged lid, placing the sprigs of thyme between them.
3 Cover with oil. Store in the refrigerator and allow to mellow for a few days before using. Will keep for up to 1 week.

1 pint (600ml) thick set yogurt (not Greek)
sea salt and freshly ground black pepper
3–4 sprigs fresh thyme
olive oil, to cover

Note
Some commercially-made yogurt is suitable for making into soft cheese but only if it is the natural unstirred variety, therefore the label should be checked carefully.

Bouquet garnis

Makes 8

butter muslin
8 bay leaves
4 teaspoons dried marjoram
4 teaspoons dried thyme
4 teaspoons dried parsley
4 teaspoons dried rosemary

1 Take a piece of muslin and cut out 8 circles approximately 4 inches (10cm) in diameter.
2 Break up a bay leaf into the centre of each piece of muslin and add ½ teaspoon of each of the other herbs. Gather the muslin round the herbs to form a bag and secure tightly with cotton or kitchen string, leaving long ends to the strings.

Gift wrap
Pack the bouquet garnis in an attractive glass jar with a stopper, then tie round with ribbon or braid.

Gift label
These little herb bags can be used to flavour soups, sauces, stocks and casseroles.

Goat cheese in olive oil

½ lb (225g) cylindrical piece of goat's cheese
5 cloves garlic, peeled and sliced
4 sprigs rosemary and thyme
1 teaspoon black peppercorns
olive oil, to cover

1 Slice the cheese into 8 equal rounds. Place in a glass preserving jar with a hinged lid.
2 Distribute the garlic, herbs and peppercorns around the cheese. Cover with oil.
3 Store in the refrigerator and allow to marinade for 24 hours before using. This will keep in the refrigerator for up to 2 weeks.

Christmas pudding

Makes one 2½ pint (1.5 litre) pudding

1 Mix together the dried fruit, cherries, peel, orange and lemon rind, breadcrumbs, flour, salt, spices, sugar, nuts and suet in a large bowl. Whisk together the orange juice, eggs, spirits and molasses and stir into the dry ingredients.
2 Turn into a 2½ pint (1.5 litre) greased pudding basin, smooth the surface and cover with a double thickness of greased greaseproof paper, with a pleat in the centre to allow for expansion, then over-wrap with foil. Tie in position with string.
3 Steam the pudding for 6 hours, adding boiling water to the steamer or saucepan as necessary. If you are using a pressure cooker, place the basin on a trivet and add 3½ pints (2 litres) of boiling water. Fit the lid and steam without pressure for 30 minutes. Bring to high pressure and cook for 2¼ hours. Reduce the pressure slowly.
4 Cool in basin. Replace the wrappings with fresh pleated greaseproof paper and foil. Store in a cool, dry place until ready for packing. Alternatively, store in the refrigerator.

Note
The pudding may be frozen for up to 1 year, provided it is not in a glass basin. Thaw at room temperature overnight, before re-steaming for serving.

Gift wrap
Leave the pudding in the basin and stand in the middle of a square of calico cloth trimmed round the edges with pinking shears. Draw edges together over the top of the pudding and tie round with red ribbon. Add a sprig of holly and attach a miniature bottle of brandy or rum for flaming.

Gift label
Store in a cool pantry or larder or refrigerator (if space permits). Re-steam for 2 hours before serving. To 'flame' the pudding put 3–4 tablespoons of brandy into a metal soup ladle and warm by holding over a gas flame, then quickly light the brandy and pour over and round the pudding.

8 oz (225g) currants
6 oz (175g) raisins
6 oz (175g) sultanas
4 oz (100g) cooking dates
2 oz (50g) undyed glacé cherries, chopped
1 oz (25g) chopped candied peel
juice and grated rind ½ orange
grated rind ½ lemon
3 oz (75g) fresh wholemeal breadcrumbs
3 oz (75g) plain wholemeal flour (85% or 100%)
pinch sea salt
1 teaspoon ground mixed spice
½ teaspoon ground cinnamon
½ teaspoon freshly grated nutmeg
2 oz (50g) dark muscovado sugar
2 oz (50g) split almonds, chopped
4 oz (100g) vegetable suet (available at good health food stores)
2 free-range eggs
2 tablespoons brandy
2 tablespoons port
2 tablespoons rum
1 tablespoon molasses

Miniature puddings

For people living alone, make miniature Christmas puddings in teacups or small basins (see recipe on page 99). To improve the flavour, prick the base of the pudding and spoon over a tablespoon of brandy. Store, wrapped in greaseproof paper and foil.

Mild ale

This simple recipe for beer uses dried hops, obtainable from a home-brew shop or some chemists.

1 lb (450g) jar malt extract
1 gallon (4.5 litres) water,
   preferably filtered
1 oz (25g) dried hops
   (Goldings)
1 teaspoon dried yeast
clear honey

1 Wash and rinse a 3.3 gallon (15 litre) white plastic bucket. Warm the jar of malt extract in a pan of hot water so that it will pour cleanly into the fermenting bucket, then add 2 pints (1 litre) of warm water and stir with a long-handled spoon until dissolved.

2 Put $7/_8$ of the hops into a clean muslin bag. Bring 6 pints (3.5 litres) of water to the boil, add the bag of hops and boil hard for 30 minutes.

3 After removing the muslin bag, pour the liquid from the pan into the 'wort' in the bucket. When tepid, sprinkle the yeast over. Put the remaining hops in a muslin bag and drop into the bucket to infuse during fermentation. Cover with a lid. Keep at room temperature for about one week, until fermentation stops. After 48 hours, skim off the head.

4 Siphon off the brew into screw-top beer bottles, leaving 1 inch (2.5cm) headroom at the top. 'Prime' at the rate of 1–1¼ teaspoons of honey per 2 pints (1 generous litre). Too much honey will cause the beer to explode or be too frothy to pour. Too little will make it flat and lifeless. Screw on the tops and store upright at room temperature for about 10 days. Drink well chilled.

Note
When pouring out beer take care not to shake up the yeast sediment. Hold the bottle up to the light to gauge this and pour steadily, without shaking, into a jug, stopping just before the dark sludge slides out.

Gift mince pies

Makes 16

Attractive mince pies, made with sugar-free mincemeat
(see page 97) and decorated with pastry holly leaves or
a star.

For the pastry
12 oz (350g) fine plain
wholemeal pastry flour
pinch sea salt (optional)
6 oz (175g) soft vegetable
margarine, or a mixture of
white vegetable fat with
unsalted butter
cold water, to mix
1 small free-range egg,
beaten or milk for glazing

For the filling
about 14 oz (400g) sugar-free
mincemeat

1 Sift the flour into a mixing bowl and add the bran
remaining in the sieve. If you are using salt, stir it into
the flour. Rub in the margarine (or butter and margarine)
until the mixture resembles fine breadcrumbs. Add
enough cold water to mix to a soft, but not sticky, dough.
2 Roll out the pastry to ⅛ inch (3mm) thick and cut 16
bases with a 3½ inch (9cm) fluted cutter and 16 lids with
a 2½ inch (6.5cm) fluted cutter. If wished, cut out stars
in half the lids with a 1 inch (2.5cm) star cutter.
3 Line 2½ inch (6.5cm) patty tins with the bases and
fill with a heaped teaspoon of mincemeat. Dampen the
pastry edges and cover with the lids. Make a small
steamhole in the centre of the plain mince pies and
decorate with pastry holly leaves and berries made from
the trimmings.
4 Brush the tops with beaten egg or milk to glaze. Bake
in a preheated moderately hot oven, 200°C (400°F/Gas
Mark 6), for about 20 minutes. Turn out on wire racks
to cool. When completely cold store the mince pies in
an airtight tin and leave until ready for packing.

Note
The mince pies can be frozen before cooking; freeze them in the tin
if you can spare it, otherwise remove them when solid and pack
carefully. Replace them in the tin to bake.

Gift wrap
Arrange on a pretty plate lined with silver or gold doilies. Wrap with
clear Cellophane and add a Christmas gift tag.

Carob Easter eggs

use approximately 6 oz
(175g) plain no-added-
sugar carob bar per 5½
inch (14cm) high eggs

To decorate
thin pieces of ribbon
Easter chicks

1 Polish the inside of the mould with a soft dry cloth so that the surface of the carob will be glossy.

2 Melt the carob in a double boiler or in a bowl placed over a pan of simmering water. Spoon some into the mould, tilting it to coat the inside completely. If you have too much, pour it out before it sets; if you have too little, quickly spoon in some more.

3 Place the mould upside-down on a sheet of greaseproof or waxed paper and leave in a cold place to set (not a refrigerator).

4 When the carob is set, it should start to shrink away from the side of the mould; if this has not happened return the mould to a cool place and allow to harden further. Gently ease off the mould, then make the second half of the shell (it is quicker to buy two Easter egg moulds of course).

5 Fill one half of the shell with carob-coated dates (see page 81) carob-dipped dried fruit or carob 'buttons', then fill the top half with crumpled parchment paper, to prevent them getting damaged. Join the two halves by brushing the rims with melted carob and pressing them gently together. Tie a ribbon to secure.

Note
Plastic and metal moulds can be obtained from most good kitchen shops.

Gift wrap
The eggs would make a lovely present in a small wicker basket filled with a 'nest' of shredded tissue paper. Decorate with silk flowers, bows and ribbons or ornamental Easter chicks, depending whether you are making them for a child or an adult.

Solid carob eggs

Makes 6

1 With a needle, very carefully pierce a tiny hole in each end of the egg shell and blow out the contents of the egg into a bowl. Enlarge one hole to ¼ inch (5mm) wide to take a small piping nozzle. Rinse out each shell under cold running water and leave to drain.

2 When they are dry, put a piece of sticky tape over the smaller hole in each egg so that it cannot leak.

3 Break the carob bar into a bowl and melt it over a pan of hot water. When it reaches pouring consistency, spoon into a nylon piping bag fitted with a small nozzle and pipe into the egg shells through the large hole; you may have to enlarge the hole a little. Swirl it round from time to time to remove any air bubbles. Leave the eggs overnight to set.

4 Carefully crack the eggs and peel off the shells. Decorate with narrow ribbons, sticking them on with a little melted carob. Alternatively, wrap each egg tightly in coloured foil.

6 empty egg shells (see method opposite)
1 lb (450g) plain no-added-sugar carob bar

Gift wrap
A cardboard egg tray provides an obvious seasonal container for small Easter eggs nestling on a bed or 'straw' made out of fine strands of coloured tissue paper. Do not forget to over-wrap the tray and eggs with clear Cellophane paper. In the weeks approaching Easter, egg cups and small ceramic dishes shaped with chicks or small rabbits become available in the shops. These are ideal for filling with small carob Easter eggs.

Carob hazelnut Christmas tree

1 lb (450g) plain no-added-sugar carob bars, broken into pieces
8 oz (225g) roasted hazelnuts, coarsely chopped (see page 80)
extra carob for assembling the tree, about 2 oz (50g)
8-inch (20cm) thin round silver cake board
1 Brazil nut

1 Put the carob pieces into a large heatproof bowl over a saucepan of barely simmering water and leave until the carob has melted, stirring occasionally.

2 Remove the bowl from the pan. Stir in the coarsely chopped hazelnuts and mix well.

3 Meanwhile, line three large baking sheets with foil (any flat tray, upturned cake tin or pieces of heavy cardboard can be used). It is important the surface is level and rigid enough so that the branches do not bend while they are setting.

4 Mark ten crosses on the foil, leaving about 1 inch (2.5cm) between each cross. The measurements for each bar of the crosses are: 2½ inches (6.5cm); 3 inches (7.5cm); 3½ inches (9cm); 4½ inches (11.5cm); 5 inches (13cm); 5½ inches (14cm); 6 inches (15cm); 6½ inches (16.5cm); 7 inches (18cm); 7½ inches (19cm).

5 To make the branches, drop teaspoonfuls of the mixture along the marked bars of the crosses, starting from the largest size and working to the smallest. Leave to set at room temperature.

6 For the base of the tree, you will need an 8-inch (20cm) thin round silver cake board or a piece of heavy cardboard covered with decorative silver paper or foil (it must be rigid and strong enough to support all the branches of the tree).

7 Melt extra carob over simmering water. To assemble the tree, join the ten crosses in pairs, starting from the largest and working down to the smallest by dropping about a teaspoon of the melted carob into the centre of the base cross. It may be necessary to move the top cross around until the best position is found; if branches look a little uneven, support underneath with a match box.

8 When each pair of crosses is set, place the largest pair on the silver cake board, joining with melted carob as before. It is important that each section is completely set before topping with another pair of crosses.

9 When the tree is assembled, cut an end off the Brazil

nut, so it will sit neatly on the top of the tree. Dip in melted carob, then position on top of the tree. If liked, dust the tree lightly with sifted carob powder.

Note
Do not use a blender or food processor for chopping the nuts as they will be chopped too finely.

Gift wrap
Pack in a large cardboard box. Surround the tree with crumpled tissue paper to avoid breakage, then cover with cling-film or a lid. Decorate with a bow of satin ribbon and a sprig of holly.

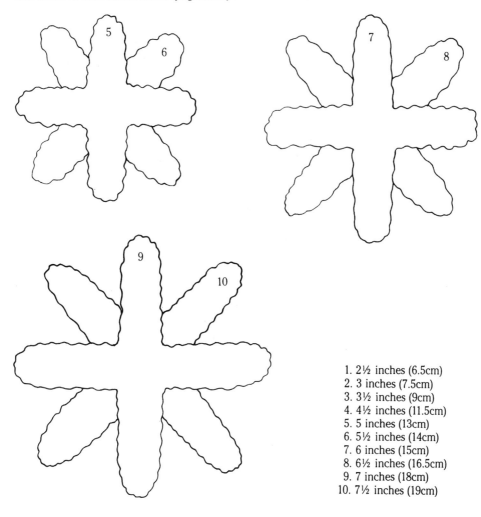

1. 2½ inches (6.5cm)
2. 3 inches (7.5cm)
3. 3½ inches (9cm)
4. 4½ inches (11.5cm)
5. 5 inches (13cm)
6. 5½ inches (14cm)
7. 6 inches (15cm)
8. 6½ inches (16.5cm)
9. 7 inches (18cm)
10. 7½ inches (19cm)

Carob-dipped strawberries

These are best eaten the same day, so they make a good present to take with you to a dinner party.

approximately 6 oz (175g) plain no-added-sugar carob bar, broken into pieces
1 lb (450g) strawberries

1 Melt the carob in a bowl or top of a double boiler set over a pan of simmering water. Remove from the heat, but keep over hot water. (If the carob thickens, return to the heat and stir until smooth.)
2 Holding each strawberry by its stalk, dip the bottom half into the melted carob. Allow the excess to drain back into the bowl, then carefully lay on greaseproof paper and leave in a cool place to dry.
3 Place in paper sweet-cases. Store, covered, in the refrigerator. (Do not store for more than 24 hours as they are at their best up to 12 hours after the carob has set.)

Note
Strawberries should not be washed but should be wiped instead with a clean cloth.

Variations
A variety of different fruits are suitable, including grapes, cherries, peeled lychees and mandarin segments. Choose ripe but firm fruit, free from any blemish. If the fruit has a stalk, such as a cherry, leave it on. Make sure the fruit is clean and dry, and dip each one in melted carob, holding it by the stalk if it has one, otherwise use a cocktail stick.

Home-made mayonnaise

Makes ½ pint (300ml)

1 Put the egg in a blender or food processor with the lemon juice, salt, pepper and 1 tablespoon of oil; process until the mixture is fluffy, about 10 seconds.
2 With the motor running, add the oil in a thin, steady stream through the feed tube. (When the mixture begins to thicken, the rest of the oil can be added more quickly.) Process until all the oil is incorporated and the mayonnaise is thick and glossy. Taste and check the seasoning.
3 Pour into a clean container, cover. Store in the refrigerator for up to 7 days.

1 free-range egg
juice ½ lemon
¼ level teaspoon sea salt
plenty of freshly ground
    black pepper
½ pint (300ml) grapeseed oil

Variations
Use olive oil, or ¼ pint (150ml) each olive and sunflower oils.

Note
All the ingredients must be at room temperature. If the mixture should curdle, switch off the machine and transfer the curdled mixture to a jug or basin. Put another egg in the blender or processor and gradually pour in the curdled mixture, then the remaining oil.

Citrus pomanders

Not really food, except that they are made from things to be found in the kitchen, citrus pomanders make beautiful Christmas gifts.

2 large oranges
approximately 3 oz (75g) cloves, to cover
2 teaspoons each ground cinnamon, nutmeg, cloves and allspice
1 tablespoon orris root powder
various trimmings, for decoration

1 If you want to make a hanging pomander stick ½-inch (5mm) wide Sellotape round the orange at right angles, then fill in the gaps with cloves (do not insert them too close together, or some will be pushed out as the orange dries and shrinks). Remove the tape and you will have neat channels along which to place the ribbon.

2 Roll the orange in the spiced mixture; then rub it all over with orris root powder to make sure the scent is well fixed.

3 Wrap it in tissue paper and place in a warm, dark place such as an airing cupboard for 6–8 weeks until it is hard and dry.

4 Unwrap and shake or blow off the surplus powder. Tie pretty ribbons or cord around the orange so that it can be hung up in a wardrobe, or cupboard. Decorate with lace, dried flowers or any pretty knick-knack. It will keep its scent for years, becoming increasingly shrunken and wizened.

Variations
Choose unblemished lemons or limes instead of the oranges.

Note
You can work directly into the fruit, but if the skin is rather thick the clove tops may break. If this happens, make the holes with cocktail sticks first.

Essence of vanilla

12 fl oz (350ml) brandy
1 vanilla pod, split vertically

1 Pour the brandy into a pretty glass bottle, stoppered with a cork for preference. Drop the vanilla pod into the bottle and seal tightly.

2 Store in a cool, dark place for at least 6 weeks before using.

Gift label
This vanilla essence may be used sparingly to flavour whipped cream, baked fruit and sweet sauces, or to moisten mincemeat and Christmas cakes. Fill up with more brandy when half used.

Note
If making for presents, the cork can be sealed with red or green sealing wax.

Index